BECOMING ORTHODOX

—REVISED EDITION—

BECOMING ORTHODOX

A Journey to the Ancient Christian Faith

Peter E. Gillquist

Conciliar Press
Ben Lomond, California

Original edition was published by Wolgemuth & Hyatt, Publishers, Inc.
First printing, August 1989
Second printing, February 1990
Third printing, December 1990

Revised edition published by Conciliar Press
P.O. Box 76
Ben Lomond, California 95005-0076

Unless otherwise noted, all Scripture quotations are from the New King James Version of the Bible, © 1979, 1980, 1982, 1984 by Thomas Nelson, Inc., Nashville, Tennessee, and are used by permission.

Quotations noted NASB are from the New American Standard Bible, copyrighted by the Lockman Foundation © 1960, 1962, 1963, 1968, 1971, 1972, 1973, 1975, 1977, and are used by permission.

Library of Congress Cataloging-in-Publication Data

Gillquist, Peter E.
    Becoming Orthodox: a journey to the ancient Christian faith /
Peter E. Gillquist. —Rev. ed.
        p. cm.
        ISBN 0-9622713-3-0: $10.95
1. Antiochian Evangelical Orthodox Mission—History. 2. Evangelical Orthodox Church—History. 3. Antiochian Orthodox Christian Archdiocese of North America—History. 4. Orthodox Eastern Church—United States—History. 5. Orthodox Eastern Church—Doctrines. 6. Gillquist, Peter E. I. Title.
BX738.A743G55   1992
281.9'73—dc20   92-40423
                                                                          CIP

To His Eminence,
Metropolitan PHILIP Saliba

You said in Detroit in 1987
that if you had to receive
the Evangelical Orthodox into
the Archdiocese again, you would
do it a million times.

On behalf of us all, we'd
say Yes again, a million times!
God grant you *many* years.

CONTENTS

Foreword to the Revised Edition

February 15, 1987, was a glorious day for the Holy Orthodox Church of Christ. Sixty new priests and deacons, along with two hundred new Orthodox faithful, joined the ranks of Holy Orthodoxy at the Saint Nicholas Antiochian Orthodox Cathedral of Los Angeles. Metropolitan Philip Saliba presided over the moving ceremonies.

The people who comprise the clergy and laity of the Antiochian Evangelical Orthodox Mission (AEOM) came to Holy Orthodoxy and to the Antiochian Archdiocese in North America from a varied—but on the whole, evangelical Protestant—background. Many of these Orthodox missionary clergy were formerly the leaders and "stars" of Campus Crusade for Christ.

Their venture into Holy Orthodoxy is indeed very moving. As staff directors of the Campus Crusade for Christ, they were unhappy they had no Church to which they could send those people who converted to Christ through their efforts. While sending these new converts back to their own Churches and denominations, the evangelists realized that this was not the true solution.

So they asked themselves: What happened to the Church which Christ founded? For they preferred instead to send their converts to such a New Testament Church. The question is very basic. Is there a Church which today meets the criteria of Christ's Church?

The group of campus evangelists decided to separate and research the question independently; at an appointed hour, they would then meet again to share their findings.

When they met together to exchange their information, to their amazement they were all in agreement.

They found that the Church of Christ, as described and depicted in the ancient documents pertaining to the life and practice of the early Church, was a Church that was Eucharistic, evangelical, and missionary. They also discovered that bishops were important figures in the life of this Church. The bishops represented Christ and the Apostles; they presided over the Eucharist, "teaching aright the word of truth" through a special *charisma veritatis* given to them. The bishops essentially guaranteed the unity of both the local and the universal catholic Church. Presiding over the *one* Eucharist of the *one* Church, the bishops' interdependence in communion with one another was the pattern of Christian unity and united Christian mission to the world given to the Church since apostolic times.

In searching for this Church, they reviewed the history of Christendom and realized that at the time of the great councils (A.D. 325-787), the Truth was with the Church of these councils. It is this Church which was later known as the "Byzantine Church."

At the time of the split between Eastern and Western Christianity in the eleventh century, the researchers easily discerned that there was deviation from the mind, life, and practice of the universal catholic Church in the West. This was evident in at least two cases: the procession of the Holy Spirit from the Father only (the West introduced the teaching of the procession of the Spirit from the Father "and the Son," *filioque*); and the form of Church government, which is conciliar and participatory, based upon the integrity of the local Church, where the catholic Church is to be found. The researchers had no difficulty in realizing that on both counts, the only body which meets the criteria of the Church founded by Christ, the Church of apostolic tradition, faith, and practice, is today's Holy Orthodox Church of Christ.

As the campus evangelists searched for this Church, they were led to the "onion-domed" Slavic Churches, and then to the Greek. They had lengthy talks and honest conversations with today's exponents of the Church which they identified as the Church which Christ founded.

Rejoicing at some of their contemporary finds, their research brought them grave disappointment at other discoveries. It is true that nothing human is perfect, and that today, as in the past, human factors continue to play both a positive and a negative role in the life of the Church founded by Christ. In spite of all this, the evangelicals decided to get off the fence, to jump into the Church, and to do it with both feet. They have done this, and their present commitment to Orthodox mission and evangelism is very promising.

Anyone who participates in the annual Conference on Missions and Evangelism over the Labor Day weekend each year will agree with the following: the "Evangelical Orthodox" have resurrected the essential dimension of evangelism in the life of the Church for the Holy Orthodox! Unfortunately, this dimension has not always been well emphasized in the past, not even in the present!

One of the main concerns of today's Orthodox Church, especially in the lands of the so-called "diaspora," is Orthodox unity and a united missionary front. The former Evangelical Orthodox can certainly fully participate and provide new strength to this endeavor of a united Orthodox mission in North America.

This book by Fr. Peter Gillquist, *Becoming Orthodox*, tells us of the venture of these former evangelical Protestants. It describes the problems they encountered and the questions they had to answer for themselves and for the people who followed them. This account also details their final entrance into full communion with canonical Orthodoxy and their ambition to "make America Orthodox"!

This present edition of the book concludes with an added epilogue, an account of the more recent life and work of the Antiochian Evangelical Orthodox Mission.

Father Gillquist's work is indeed very exciting, both from an historical and from a theological point of view. The reader, whether Orthodox or not, will enjoy reading about this exciting adventure of people who were searching for the New Testament Church, and who were able to pursue their heroic commitment to truth, no matter how great the obstacles in finding the way to follow this commitment by joining canonical Orthodoxy.

The reader will certainly appreciate the frankness, the evangelical and apostolic simplicity and freshness with which this book has been written. I highly recommend it to all.

September 14, 1992
Feast of the Exaltation of
the Holy Cross

MAXIMOS AGHIORGOUSSIS, TH.D.
Bishop of Pittsburgh
Greek Orthodox Archdiocese

Acknowledgments

I wish to acknowledge the work of Fr. Jon Braun in chapter 4, "Finding the New Testament Church;" Fr. Richard Ballew in chapter 7, "Call No Man Father;" and Fr. Weldon Hardenbrook in chapter 9, "A Sign for All Christians." (These chapters are based upon works previously published in booklet form by Conciliar Press).

My thanks to Mr. David Heim, managing editor of the *Christian Century*, for permission to adapt much of the *Epilogue* from my article "Evangelicals Turned Orthodox" (March 4, 1992).

My sincere appreciation to Frs. Gordon Walker, Jack Sparks, Gregory Rogers, Joseph Allen, to Michael Hyatt and Tom and Joann Webster for reviewing the first edition manuscript. My thanks also to Mrs. Shirley Dillon for her tireless typing of the initial manuscript through several drafts. And finally, my thanks to those who edited and proofread the new edition.

PETER E. GILLQUIST
Santa Barbara, California

PART ONE

FROM ARROWHEAD SPRINGS TO ANTIOCH

1

NEVER SAY NEVER

"Not in your lifetime, not in my lifetime, have we ever witnessed such a mass conversion to holy Orthodoxy," announced Metropolitan Philip Saliba as he began his sermon at Saint Nicholas Cathedral in Los Angeles that February morning in 1987.

In truth, it was *afternoon*. With the ordination of sixty of us to the diaconate and the priesthood, plus the receiving of nearly two hundred lay people, the service had already taken up over four hours!

Priests and lay leaders had come from all over North America to witness the event. Friends and family came to take part. Bishop Maximos of the Pittsburgh diocese of the Greek Orthodox Church was present and spoke at the banquet which followed.

It had been an entire week of festivity. The receiving of new members and ordinations had begun the week before, February 8, at Saint Michael's Church in the Los Angeles suburb of Van Nuys. Those to be ordained priests this day, February 15, had been ordained deacons a week earlier. In the Orthodox Church, you do not go from lay status to the priesthood in a single step.

"Last week I said to the evangelicals, 'Welcome home!' " the Archbishop continued. "Today I am saying, 'Come home, *America!* Come home to the faith of Peter and Paul.' "

I looked across the large expanse of the altar area at the cathedral and into the eyes of the threescore others who had, with me, just received the grace of ordination to holy orders. The smell of incense lingered from the celebration of the Divine Liturgy, and the candles on the huge marble altar were still aglow.

Many of the Orthodox priests who had come such a great distance to participate had tears in their eyes, as did many of us newcomers to the Church. "Our fathers brought Orthodoxy to America," whispered the veteran priest James Meena of his Arabic Christian forebears. Then he smiled and added, "Now it's your turn to bring America to Orthodoxy."

Why would America need Orthodox Christianity, or even be remotely interested in it? It's so old, so foreign, so "Catholic," so complicated. Could it ever, as we say, play in Peoria?

But second, and of even more immediate concern, whatever would possess two thousand Bible-believing, blood-bought, Gospel-preaching, Christ-centered, lifelong evangelical Protestants to come to embrace this Orthodox faith so enthusiastically? Is this a new form of religious rebellion? Have vital Spirit-filled Christian people somehow jumped the track to a staid and lifeless, crusty, sacral gloom? Worse yet, is this one of those subtle deceptions of the enemy?

Those of us who led this particular journey met in the 1960s in Campus Crusade for Christ. Though we were products of the Fifties, we must have been something of a tip-off to the turbulent Sixties just ahead: dissatisfied—or better to say, unsatisfied—with the status quo of what we perceived as dull, denominational American Christianity.

Gutsy, outspoken, radical, hopefully maximal, we didn't like the institutional Church and we didn't like the world system, and we were out to change them both.

What great days they were! We wouldn't trade them for anything. And we would not trade where we are now for anything. The one certainly led us to the other.

The Challenge of the Campus

"There's one campus in America you guys can *never* crack," an evangelical businessman friend told me over lunch in Chicago one day in late 1965.

"Which one?" I shot back, already having determined in my mind that I would go there next.

"Notre Dame," he smirked.

"Bet we can," I said. We finished eating over small talk and said goodbye.

I hurried home and telephoned the chaplain's office in South Bend. "I'd like to see him just as soon as possible," I told the secretary after identifying myself.

"I have an appointment for you to see Father at nine tomorrow morning," she said after checking his schedule.

"Good. I'll be there."

That's the way we were. The greater the challenge, the higher the mark on the wall, the better we liked it. And the better we performed. I threw some clothes in a suitcase, said goodbye to my wife and children, pulled out of our snow-packed driveway in Evanston and headed down Outer

Drive toward South Bend. I checked into a motel adjacent to the campus with a prayer that the doors to the Irish would somehow be open.

A few months later we had probably twenty-five hundred students from Notre Dame and the adjacent Saint Mary's College packed into the brand-new Convocation Center on campus, for two nights in a row, to hear Jon Braun and the New Folk, our preaching/singing team. I had promised the chaplain, "We're not coming to make Protestants out of your students, but to call them to a deeper commitment to Jesus Christ." And I meant every word of it.

The response was incredible. In those days, we passed out 3"x 5"cards and asked our listeners to put a check mark by their names if they had prayed with us to open up their lives to Christ. Over two hundred had checked.

We had cracked Notre Dame.

Then came Cal Berkeley. "The Berkeley Blitz," we called it. That was the winter of the 1966-67 school year. We decided we had had enough of the free-speech movement and Betina Apthecker. "Let's hit the campus and shake it to the core," we told each other. Hundreds of students— Berkeley students!—gave up their lunch hour to hear Billy Graham speak in the Greek Theater on campus, following his earlier breakfast meeting with scores of faculty members. Jon Braun spoke on the steps of Sproul Hall the next morning and actually shut down a heckler from the crowd. Nobody else would challenge him, and we won.

Though there were not the ongoing results we had hoped for at Berkeley, at least we had engaged the radicals on their own turf and had succeeded in doing what we had set out to do.

At once, we loved it and we hated it. A shock-troop mentality is thrilling fun, but it can also bring deep disappointment. Though we exhibited some of the same boldness we saw in the early Christians in the Book of Acts, we found nowhere near the long-term staying power in those we reached. Most of the decisions for Christ honestly did not stick.

Our Growing Frustration

Our slogan was "Win the Campus for Christ Today— Win the World for Christ Tomorrow." As much as we loathed to admit it, while we were busy winning the campus, the world was getting worse. We had established Campus Crusade chapters on many of the major campuses in America during the decade of the Sixties, but it was precisely in those same Sixties that our nation's campuses came unglued. They unraveled morally, politically, and culturally. We had done our job, and things got worse, not better. The campus world of 1970 was far, far less culturally Christian than the campus world of 1960.

"What we are doing is not working," we admitted to each other. "We get the decisions, we get the commitments to Christ, we are building the organization and recruiting the staff, but we are not producing a change. We are a failure in the midst of our own success."

Dr. Jack Sparks couldn't get his mind off Berkeley. He had been a professor teaching statistics and research design at Penn State and at the University of Northern Colorado before he joined the Campus Crusade staff to direct a systematic follow-up program of literature through computerized distribution. Now, after the blitz, he asked for and got a few hard-core Campus Crusade staff people to join him, and he took off for the Berkeley campus.

He out-radicalized all the rest of us. He swapped his business suits for denim overalls and work shirts, grew a beard, and hit the campus with a higher commitment to Christ than the radicals had ever had to their causes. He even baptized some of his converts in the famous fountain on the Berkeley campus mall!

The style he used, the literature he produced, and the life he and his wife Esther lived crossed over the new counter-culture barriers and began to produce something that gave promise of permanence. It bordered on something you would see in the Book of Acts. It looked less and less like Campus Crusade, and more and more like the beginnings of a Christian community—or dare I say, a Church.

2

THE PHANTOM SEARCH FOR THE PERFECT CHURCH

I had been raised in a mainline denominational Church in Minneapolis. Among my earliest desires as a child was the desire to follow God. Sunday school and Church were a given on Sunday morning. Even the non-serious kids rarely cut. I never disbelieved in God that I recall. I just got bored somewhere along the way.

Through grade school, we sat with our parents. By junior high, the "precious young people," as the older adults often called us, sat together. And as we grew older, we moved farther and farther back.

In high school, I was elected president of the youth group. That meant I had to lead devotions on Sunday night, and I felt empty. "I'm not sure I'm even a Christian anymore," I told my friend, who was president the year ahead of me.

"You're miles ahead of me," he responded. "I don't believe there's a God." And he had been one of the most vigorous and active kids in the whole congregation!

In 1956, after high school, I enrolled across town at the University of Minnesota. The following year, I joined the Sigma Alpha Epsilon fraternity and moved on campus. The fraternity house was right next door to our denominational student center, and I remember vowing I would never set foot in the place. I never did. It was not that I hated God or even the Church. Simply, the Church no longer did anything for me. It scratched a place that didn't itch. So I quit going. And nobody ever came after me.

Except Campus Crusade for Christ.

The local "Crusade" man was systematically speaking in all the fraternities on campus, and ours was on the list. By now it was 1959, and our chapter president, a Roman Catholic, had invited a different religious speaker in every Monday night during Lent to help straighten up the level of life in the fraternity. The Crusade team was a part of that series.

A New Commitment

When I heard these people stand up and unashamedly tell what Jesus Christ meant to them, the message rang a resonant chord somewhere down inside me. My girlfriend, Marilyn, had already made a firm commitment of her life to Christ a month earlier, and I knew I would have to do the same thing. I helped the Crusade leader start a weekly Bible study in the fraternity. And after about three or four weeks, I committed myself to Christ in prayer one night after the evening Bible study when everyone else had gone to bed. I knew I meant business in my decision to follow Him, no matter what the cost.

Shortly afterwards—and I don't recall which happened first—I took the Crusade leader to a Lutheran Church, and he took me to his independent Baptist Church. He had me tell the story of my recent conversion before a large Sunday school group. But even more memorable was the morning I persuaded him to go with me. We went to a Lutheran Church in downtown Minneapolis and listened to what I felt was an excellent sermon on living for Christ.

On the way out the door, he turned and said to me, "Well, I'm going to have to go home and eat."

"What do you mean?" I asked.

"The Bible is the sincere milk of the Word, and I'm starving to death," he said.

"You mean you didn't like the service?" I asked.

"There just was no solid content to it, no verse-by-verse Bible teaching," he said with a frown.

"But you heard what the pastor said about Christ," I said. "I felt he did a good job."

"Well, your discernment will grow as you get to know the Lord better," he said. "We have got to have in-depth Bible teaching in order to grow in our faith."

How could I argue with that? I started devouring the New Testament.

In the months that followed, I came to love Christ more and more, and the organized Church less and less. Though not every one in Campus Crusade believed as our staff leader did, through his influence I came to reject communion and baptism as sacraments through which the grace of God comes to us, and I embraced a more privatized faith in God. In fact, a year later I was rebaptized at my own request by a Baptist minister in Dallas. I was sure my infant baptism had not "taken."

Preferring the warmth and intimacy and enthusiasm of Campus Crusade meetings to the rigidity of Sunday worship, I found myself moving from my past experience of Church without Christ to the very opposite: Christ without Church. Only later was I to discover that neither will carry you for the long haul.

That summer I attended a Campus Crusade conference on the outskirts of the Twin Cities. It was there I met a number of the men with whom I would serve God for the rest of my life. Dick Ballew and his wife Sylvia had pulled in a day late because their car had broken down somewhere between Texas and Minneapolis. He stood and told how he was able to introduce the garage mechanic to Christ—right on the spot. *Boy, that's it!* I thought to myself. *That's what I want to be able to do.*

The Years of Preparation

By my senior year in college I had set as my goal to devote my life to the ministry, perhaps even in the institutional Church. One morning I drove across the river to Saint Paul and visited the campus of a nearby denominational seminary. There was an older professor on the faculty who was known as a very godly man. I went to see him and told him my story of growing up in the Church, straying away, and then coming back to faith in Christ at the University. "I feel God is calling me to the ministry and wonder about coming here for my seminary work," I volunteered as I ended my saga.

Tears came into his eyes. "I pray for young men like you to come here to seminary," he said. "But don't come. Go somewhere else. Here they'll talk you out of everything you have come to believe." I was unaware then that what I would come to know as "Protestant liberalism" was in its heyday at many of the major denominational seminaries. I enrolled at Dallas Theological Seminary in Dallas, Texas, and I promise you, it wasn't liberal!

My time at Dallas absolutely settled for me the issue of the inspiration of the Bible. Though I had not experienced any real personal crisis over the question, at Dallas we learned why the Bible was inspired, what the Scriptures claim about themselves, and the importance of reading and believing the Scriptures. During that first year in seminary, Marilyn, my new bride, and I lived across the street from Southern Methodist University where she took her junior year of college. I started the Campus Crusade program at SMU.

The following year, I was asked to consider moving to Chicago to begin Campus Crusade at Northwestern University in Evanston, to develop a Chicago-area board, and to recruit staff at Wheaton College. I asked the registrar at Dallas, later its president, Donald Campbell, for support in leaving seminary after one year to transfer to Wheaton Graduate School. He gave me his blessing, and we moved to the Windy City in the summer of 1961 to begin our work.

It was at Wheaton that I resumed the process of disenchantment with Church. I had now been educated against anything with sacramental and liturgical overtones both in Campus Crusade and at Dallas Seminary. There were a few "weirdos" or "rebels" at Wheaton who wore wire-rimmed glasses and tweed sport coats and opted for the Episcopal Church. Most of the rest of us leaned toward what had become a growing American phenomenon: the Bible Church. I was drawn to the preaching and biblical exposition. And the singing—though sometimes glitzy—was at least energetic and alive. There were times both Marilyn and I wanted a bit more dignity, or maybe majesty, in the Sunday morning services, but giving up more meaningful worship was the trade-off for the preaching of the Bible.

One fraternity brother had, before I left college, accused me of buying into "bargain basement Christianity." I cringed when he said it because I suspected he could be right. But what was the alternative? The more I studied about liberalism in the mainline Churches, the more fearful I became of *ever* swapping Bible preaching for beauty in worship.

Occasionally Marilyn and I would visit a denominational parish, such as an evangelical Lutheran or Presbyterian Church, and be drawn back toward more serious worship. But we would balk at joining because eight or ten blocks down the street would be another Church of that same denomination where the pastor would call into question the resurrection of Christ or His virgin birth or other basics of the Christian faith. We had experienced too much of the reality of a personal walk with Christ, the joy of believing, and love for the Scriptures to ever want to be part of something disbelieving, dead, or dull. It was exciting to be a committed Christian, and I determined that nothing was going to interfere with that.

After a year at Wheaton, we moved up to Evanston to devote ourselves full time for the next six years to campus outreach at Northwestern University. We encountered fierce resistance from the campus religious community, who saw us as a threat to the established denominational student groups. Neither our evangelical beliefs nor our parachurch identity were welcomed. Nonetheless, in the mid-Sixties we finally succeeded in establishing Campus Crusade as a recognized campus group at Northwestern.

Our teams of staff and students spent their hours speaking in the various campus living groups and talking with students about Christ, individually over Cokes or coffee. We became the fastest-growing Christian group on campus. Some tolerance for us began to emerge because we were determined to play by the rules, but heated theological disagreements still remained. We were seen as sheep stealers and fundamentalists. But evangelism was getting into my blood; bringing people to Christ brought incredible fulfillment and inner reward.

"The Pipe"

Each summer, all the U.S. Campus Crusade staff would come together for staff training at Arrowhead Springs, our headquarters near San Bernardino, California. We who were area and regional directors grew to be inseparable. Having fought the wars alone on the campus all year long, we would count the days until we could take a respite together at Arrowhead Springs for the summer program. We ate together, played handball together, preached together, swam and steam-bathed together, and studied the Scriptures together.

It came to be called, "the pipe." It seemed as we would open the Scriptures together, the Holy Spirit would speak to us as one man, constantly drawing us to the mercy of God—*and back to the Church*. "Why aren't we Church?" we would ask. "Here in the New Testament, the only thing Jesus ever started was the Church." We loved what we were doing, but in the Book of Acts it was Church, not parachurch.

The summer of 1966 came to be the turning point. Jon Braun was our new National Field Coordinator; Dick Ballew was the Eastern Regional Director; Jim Craddock had the South; Robert Andrews the West; and I had the North—the Big Ten Region. Out of our zeal to discover New Testament Christianity, we decided to meet at 6:00 for breakfast every morning that summer at Sages Restaurant in downtown San Bernardino. Often Gordon Walker, our African Director, and Ken Berven, our Canadian Director, would join us. We would expect "the pipe" to open, for God to speak to us through the

Scriptures, most often the New Testament Epistles.

We pored through the New Testament, watching for passages on the grace of God and on the Church. That summer we became convinced that whatever form it would take, ultimately we would have to be Church. We viewed the Church as the place where God's grace and mercy would be manifest. We saw that each believer had gifts to bring, that the entire body of Christ could function, not just one or two paid professionals. The Church was to be a *community*.

We were taken with the fact that in the New Testament the Church began in homes, that church buildings themselves did not seem to come until the third century. Though we were never obsessed with miracles as such, all of us yearned for a place where true healing could take place and legitimate prophetic words could be uttered, where each member could "do his own thing." And we wanted a home where those who hurt could receive care and where the "un-cool" of society were every bit as important as the star running backs, the homecoming queens, and the student body presidents. The more we immersed ourselves in the New Testament, the more concerned we were becoming about the incompleteness of our being a disconnected arm of the Church.

At first, we saw an instant and simple solution to our dilemma. We would turn Campus Crusade into a Church. We knew before we started that it wouldn't fly, but we went ahead and tried anyway. It didn't fly.

In the fall of 1966, we began to build "student mobilization" groups on the campuses, groups patterned as closely as possible after our vision of the New Testament Church. We taught community, commitment, and teamwork, but stopped short of practicing baptism and communion. These groups received everything from bitter criticism from some establishment Christians to ceaseless praise from those more radical and visionary. Without meaning to be, we were on a collision course with the Campus Crusade philosophy. We could not continue this way indefinitely.

The Exodus

Ultimately, there were a number of things that caused scores of us to leave the Campus Crusade organization in 1968. As for me, I felt I had done all I could accomplish there. The parachurch wind had gone out of my sails. I wanted something more. But let me say that even to this day, I would rather present the Gospel of Jesus Christ in a college fraternity or sorority house than anywhere else on earth.

We sensed a lack of freedom. We wanted to pull out all the stops and do "everything they did in the first century" —baptize our converts, serve communion, take more vocal stands against evil. In short, we wanted above all else to be the New Testament Church.

That was it—the New Testament Church! Through the years, largely through reading the Scriptures and Church history, the passion for the New Testament Church had absolutely captured us. I'm embarrassed to recount one incident because it sounds messianic and arrogant, and in a measure it probably was.

Jon Braun and I were riding from Evanston to downtown Chicago on the elevated train one day in 1967, and I said to him, "You know what we are? We're reformers. Just like Luther and Calvin, we want to get the Church back to what it should be."

He nodded yes.

"I'm not saying we're in their league," I backtracked. "And I don't want to sound preposterous. But what we really want to do is to reform the Church."

"You're right," he agreed, and it was as though we had finally admitted it out loud to each other.

Another reason we left was that we simply believed God wanted us to. And that is what carried us through the most difficult days of our exodus. We were faced with the challenge of leaving something that was economically secure, and by now even a bit admired, to simply strike out in faith and start all over again.

It was February of 1968, and I was speaking on one of the satellite campuses of the University of Wisconsin, in La Crosse. Walking from the student union back to the dorm room where I was staying that evening, I sensed a specific nudge, a still small voice saying, "I want you to leave." When I reached the dorm, I telephoned Jon at his home in California. "I'm through," I announced, not sure what else to say.

There was a long silence on the other end. He finally said, "So am I." I mailed in my resignation letter later in the week. The exodus had begun.

Starting the Journey

That summer, we called as many of the growing numbers of the ex-staff together as we could and began preaching and teaching the New Testament Church—at least our view of it. A Lutheran Church in La Jolla, California, had allowed us use of their facilities. We didn't know how to pull off what we were calling for, but wild horses could not have slowed down our enthusiasm. "The name of the game is Church," we announced. "That's why most modern evangelism isn't changing the world. It's self-appointed, not Church-directed. People are not being reached in the context of the body of Christ—they're like newborn babies being left on a doorstep somewhere to feed and care for themselves."

One morning during the conference, I stepped outside the meeting room and spotted a young man with a button on his shirt that read, "God isn't dead—Church is." *Amen*, I said to myself. *Not only are the converts falling by the wayside, but the Churches are so pathetic they can't handle the ones who do come. The Church is in captivity to an invisible, present-day Babylon!*

So there you have it. The Church was the answer, but not any Church we had ever seen. It was the New Testament Church that we sought. And we were soon to find that countless others were looking for the same things. We were beginning what we soon began to call, *The Phantom Search for the Perfect Church!*

The easiest thing to do would have been to start a rival organization and "do it right" this time. We even had come up with a name: FOCUS, Fellowship of Christian University Students. We would out-witness, out-preach, and for sure out-church anything Campus Crusade would ever do.

But fortunately "the pipe" was still open. None of us had any peace at all with enacting such a plan. One thing was certain: we had families to feed, and there was no legitimate way to raise money to keep ourselves going as we had in the past. So most of us decided to take secular jobs.

The public relations of it all was the most difficult thing we had to face. For all the world, it looked to former cohorts as though we had left the ministry and succumbed to the pleasures and security of the world. Dick Ballew started selling coffee in Atlanta. Jon Braun briefly took a job directing a youth camp in Washington and then turned to painting houses. I stayed in Evanston for a year and began writing, then moved the following year to Memphis to work for Memphis State University.

All of us tried our hand at starting and building house

churches—with varying success and failure. We kept in touch by letter and phone.

Memphis

By the time Marilyn and I arrived in Memphis in the fall of 1969, we had four children. We purchased a large, older home in the midtown area of Memphis, specifically to have a living room big enough to hold people for Christian gatherings. I was hired as director of development at the University and executive vice president of the University foundation. Essentially a fund-raising post, the job would put me in daily touch with both University and civic leaders. Most importantly, the position kept me in first-hand contact with the student body.

When we arrived, we found a group of fifteen or twenty non-aligned Christian students on campus who ran around together and who, for a variety of reasons, did not fit within the established religious groups on the campus. These students shared that same elusive vision for the New Testament Church and desired that something be launched in that direction. Sunday evening became the appointed time, and our house the appointed place. About our only ground rule was that we would not invite new people to come. Far from being exclusive, we all felt the need to grow in our own understanding of the Church first, before we invited others to take part.

Marilyn and I made an agreement. We would not consciously seek out student leaders as we had in Campus Crusade. In an effort to see the body of Christ composed of all who would come, we simply tried to make ourselves available to any and all who showed an interest in the Christian message. It was ironic that at the end of our three years in Memphis, among those who had committed their lives to Christ were the student body president, the vice president, the AWS president, a fraternity president—*along with* some very average people, some drug dealers, prostitutes, runaways, hippies, and a broad cross-section of none of the above. Whatever mistakes we made along the way, we were clear on one thing: there could be fellowship in Christ across the entire spectrum of humanity. The variety of gifts, the variety of ministries, and the variety of effects could most certainly be experienced in Christian community.

Despite our plans not to go public in Memphis, we did. One of the girls in the Sunday night group had talked with her hairdresser about Christ, and the hairdresser asked to be baptized. She began coming Sunday nights. As bare-bones as we were, she was thrilled to be a part of a close-knit group of Christians who loved and cared for one another, and she began inviting everyone she could. We doubled in size, then tripled, and on some nights had to move out into the backyard to accommodate everyone.

The larger we grew, the less and less "Church" we were becoming. For all our desires to be otherwise, Sunday night turned into a front-lines outreach meeting which included energetic singing, an expository teaching from the Scriptures, and time in spontaneous intercessory prayer and thanksgiving. At the end of the meeting, I would often issue a call to "pray and give your life to Christ wherever you are in the room." We had served communion most every week when we were small, but as the crowd grew, those times became more infrequent. We were never sure who would be there and in what spiritual condition.

In other parts of the country, my colleagues were also pursuing the idea of house churches with varying forms and varying results. Gordon and Mary Sue Walker had moved to Mansfield, Ohio, from Columbus, and were given use of a large, working farm. For no apparent reason, runaways, hitchhikers, and other adventurers began appearing at their doorstep. Soon a small community of young men and women had grown up around them, and they began a Church in their finished basement. Gordon would baptize each of those he brought to Christ (at one retreat he baptized 26 people in an icy farm pond during a snowstorm), and weekly communion became the norm on Sunday mornings.

Harold and Barbara Dunaway were stationed with Campus Crusade in Anchorage and left the staff shortly after we did. Harold formed a board of men to underwrite his buying a former Catholic retreat house where he developed a community similar to the Mansfield group but with no connection as such. They called themselves *Maranatha North*. In the early Seventies, this group moved from a Christian fellowship gathering to the beginning stages of a Church.

Jack and Esther Sparks continued their work to impact the counter-culture in Berkeley with the message of Christ. And out of this, a house church was emerging.

The Ballews had begun a living-room church in Atlanta which finally ground to a halt. They and the Brauns both moved to the Santa Barbara area to join with the former Campus Crusade group from the University of California at Santa Barbara (UCSB) who were also chasing this dream of the True Church. This brought about a closer geographical proximity to the Sparks family who, as the hippie era died down, also moved to the community near UCSB in 1974.

Re-gathering: 1973

By the early Seventies, with most of us in different

places and largely on our own, we sensed an increased desire to work more closely together. After three years at the University, I had resigned my post and moved to the country an hour outside Memphis to restore a pre-Civil War house we had purchased. This move also allowed me to spend a bit more time as husband and father to what shortly would become six children. For upkeep, I returned to the free-lance writing I had done my last year in Evanston.

In the summer of 1973, a number of us were scheduled to be in Dallas for a week-long Christian publishers' convention. The suggestion was made that we try to pull as many of the old troops together as possible to see if we could establish at least some informal kind of network among those of us who were in the process of building New Testament house churches. About seventy men showed up.

We shared, argued, taught and fought over new insights from Scripture, and ate our meals together for the better part of a week. Everyone, it seemed, was leery of starting another new "deal" as we called it. But on the other hand, we were tired—extremely tired—of laboring alone. As the dust settled, a few of us decided we would at least relate together somewhat informally.

A few months later a group of us met at the Sparks' home in Berkeley. Without much more commonality than our desire to see the emergence of a true New Testament expression of Christianity, we decided that six of us who were forty or older would serve as "elders" of whatever it was we were going to do. I was later added as a seventh. This core group would meet together for a week once a quarter to give some oversight to this small network of Churches that we were bringing together.

Crucial also to our group was a felt need on the part of

each man to be accountable to the others and under at least some measure of visible, workable authority. During the weeks and months ahead, it dawned on us how little we knew about that which we were calling with increased frequency "the New Testament Church."

"Everybody claims to be the New Testament Church," Jack Sparks complained at one of our next gatherings. "The Catholics say they are; the Baptists say they are; the Church of Christ says it is—and nobody else is. We need to find out who's right." Sparks was such a valuable addition to us precisely because he had not had the background in evangelical higher education most of the rest of us shared. He was evangelical to the core but came in with a fresh voice and more creative questions as to what the Church was— and could be. He was not from the Bible belt and knew little of the shoptalk.

"What do you mean, 'Who's right?' " someone in the back of the room challenged. "We've got the Bible, haven't we? The way you learn about the New Testament Church is by reading the New Testament."

"Look, you're missing what I'm after," Jack replied in his compassionate way of dealing with touchy issues. "As Protestants, we know our way back to A.D. 1517 and the Reformation. As evangelicals—Bible people—we know our way up to A.D. 95 or so, when the Apostle John finished writing the Revelation. It's time we fill the gap in between."

"He's right," Gordon Walker agreed. "For the life of me, I cannot tell you the details of *where* that New Testament Church *went*."

"I'm the same way," Jon Braun added. "What I want to know is, how long did the Church remain true to Christ? In all honesty, I was taught that the minute the Apostle John drew his last breath, the Church began to head downhill. Is that really right? And if it isn't, then where and when did the Church go wrong? How could the Reformation have been avoided, anyway?"

"The way to do this, it seems to me, is to divide up areas for study," Sparks said. "For me, I'd like to take worship. I can lead a Bible study and keep the singing going, but I really struggle with leading worship. As a matter of fact, I'm not even sure what true worship really is. Are the charismatics right? Should we grab onto spontaneity and go for it? Or is there another way that Christians were called to worship?"

"Then let me do Church history," said Braun. "I want to get hold of the historic continuity of the Church—who the right Church is, who the wrong Church is, how she stayed on track or went off track."

"It's important that we get to the primary sources," Sparks exhorted. "It won't get it for us simply to read the comments of modern scholars. We've got to get right to the root documents and read through what the earliest writers had to say—the good ones and even the heretics."

"I'll take doctrine," offered Dick Ballew. "I'm sick and tired of chasing after every new spiritual emphasis that blows through town. What I want to know is what did the Church believe from the start—and what didn't it believe? I also want to look for balance. For example, what about all the weight we give to the details surrounding the second coming of Christ? Is that healthy? Did early believers do that? Sometimes I get the feeling we know more about the Second Coming than God does!

"But most important," Ballew continued, "I want to find out what the early Christians believed about Jesus Christ. What are the things that made them so willing to die for Him?"

Gordon Walker stayed silent through most of the meeting. A former Southern Baptist minister, he had been educated at the seminary in Fort Worth, Texas, and had pastored a number of Southern Baptist Churches before coming on the staff of Campus Crusade. "I'll tell you what I'm going to take," he said with a somewhat skeptical tone of voice. "I'm taking the Bible. My plan is to check out everything the rest of you brothers find out against the Bible. Because if we can't find it there, I'm not buying it."

"That's fair enough," Jon Braun said, just as things could have gotten a bit heated. "After all, that's got to be the yardstick for whatever we believe."

Ken Berven took the pre-reformation years, Ray Nethery, who resigned in 1978, the post-reformation period, and shortly afterward I was selected as our administrator.

More Than an Exercise

It would have all been academic, of course, if we had ended our discussions right there. But we weren't out just for mere facts. Two things confronted us.

First, we were now all responsible for congregations, however small. We had promised our people we would bring them into the historic mainstream of the New Testament faith. In doing so, we were not out to become one more "brand" of Christianity. Nor was our goal to stay Protestant, to become Catholic, to be Pentecostal, or to be dispensational. Our motivation was to be the best Christian people we could be, to be a twentieth-century expression of the first-century Church.

Secondly—and I cannot stress enough the importance of this decision—we had agreed on the front end to *do* and *be* whatever we found that the New Testament Church did and was, as we followed her through history. If we found we were wrong, we would change. We were committed to believe her doctrine, to enter into her worship, and to reflect her government as best we could discern it. Or to put it another way, if we found that all Christians everywhere believed a certain truth or held to a certain practice, if it was done by all and it squared with the Holy Scriptures, we would alter our course accordingly and follow the faith of our fathers.

A hermeneutic, a way of interpreting the Scriptures, was beginning to develop here. For years we had tended to view the Church in its trek through history as a sort of ranch-style structure, twenty centuries long, the foundations being re-laid in each century to reflect the culture at hand. Now, it seems, we were starting to look at the Church as a vertical structure twenty centuries high, built on the foundation of the Apostles and prophets with Christ as the cornerstone.

Instead of having to build new foundations in each generation or each century, we were struggling to see if it were possible to stay with the original apostolic foundation, with that faith once for all delivered to the saints and, in turn, to build a new floor on it for our time, to house the people of our day. We grew less and less comfortable asking, "Are the Christians in the second and third century in our Church?" The issue was more the reverse: Are we in theirs?

Few men in America or even the world, I suppose, were in a position to do the sort of work we were proposing. We were beholden to no one but the Lord and each other. We were small, free to move, and free to change. Available to adjust to what we would find, we were committed to uphold nobody's party line. We were unattached to any established Church and represented a people who had already dropped out of the structures and who were also willing to change. We had no board, no support group to tighten the purse strings if they did not like what we uncovered in Church history. All we wanted was Christ and His Church. Instead of judging history, we were inviting history to judge us.

Our basic question was, whatever happened to that Church we read about in the pages of the New Testament? Was it still around? If so, where? We wanted to be a part of it.

3

A WEEK WE WILL NOT FORGET

For me the most memorable (translate that: painful) week of our journey came in February of 1975. Ken Berven had arranged for us to use a cabin on San Juan Island in Puget Sound off the coast of Seattle. It was cold and damp outside, cold and damp inside. The cabin had what seemed like endless square feet of bare cement floor and only two beds for seven men. The oldest participant and the one with the sorest back, Ken Berven and myself, were given the beds.

This was the week we would come together and teach each other the first installment of what we were learning in the specific areas we had chosen to study.

The Worship Report

The most difficult area, I believe, for any Christian to change is how he worships on Sunday morning. The make-up of the church board can change, the pastor can be replaced, the building committee can propose alterations. But the way things go Sunday morning—whether you

are Reformed or Roman Catholic, Pentecostal or Presbyterian—had better not alter very much. Of the seven of us,
two were brought up in liturgical Churches, the rest in
moderate to informal free Churches. But all of us in our
adult years had opted for a very informal, almost spontaneous style of worship—and we had encouraged spontaneous worship in virtually all our Churches.

We felt we had an arsenal of Bible verses to back us up!
The day of Pentecost in Acts 2 always began these discussions, then on to I Corinthians 12 and 14, plus the Eutychus
incident in Acts, where Paul preached half the night. Jack
Sparks took the floor to relay to us what he had learned
about worship from the earliest accounts in the Church's
history.

"Christian worship was liturgical from the start," he
began. "The most ancient records tell us. . ."

"You've got to be kidding," I interrupted. "There's no
way that can be right."

"I'm not asking you to like what I found," Jack continued, "but the three oldest sources. . ."

"Wait," I protested again. "Are you sure you've studied
the right material? Is what you have read representative?
Not at seminary and not in my private reading have I ever
heard anyone teach that the Church was liturgical at the
start." I had always assumed that liturgy was what came
into the Church when the power of the Holy Spirit died
down.

Whatever you may say about Jack Sparks, you can
never accuse him of fudging on research. I've come to
discover that he is the best researcher I have ever met. His
credits include not only outstanding academic work
through to his Ph.D., but additional years spent working
with doctoral and post-doctoral students at Penn State.
Further, I had to admit to myself that the man had no axe to

grind. It would have been easier for him had there been no early accounts of liturgical worship because he—like me—had coached his own Church to be spontaneous in worship.

He introduced us to three early and universally recognized sources outside the Scriptures that tell us what early Christian worship was like. The source almost always considered first is the record of Saint Justin Martyr (in his *First Apology*), written around A.D. 150, where he put down on paper, for the emperor, the pattern of Christian worship. It looked like this:

SYNAXIS:
- Greeting and response
- Hymns, interspersed with
- Readings from Scripture, the "Apostles' Memoirs"
- The Homily
- Dismissal of those not in the Church

EUCHARIST:
- Greeting and response
- Intercessory Prayers
- Offertory—of bread and wine
- Consecration of Gifts
- Communion
- Giving of Thanks
- Benediction

The next document was the *Apostolic Tradition* of Hippolytus, written about A.D. 200. His writing served to back up the descriptions of worship given earlier by Saint Justin, showing these practices to be universal in the whole of the Church.

The earliest record—perhaps as early as A.D. 70 and in the heart of the New Testament era—came from the

Didache or "The Teaching of the Twelve." The reference here was particularly strong concerning the Eucharist, and was significant because it came so very early. This three-fold early witness to liturgy and sacrament stood together with the New Testament and other ancient references to form a unified account of first- and second-century worship.

"What this means," Sparks told us, "is that there were essentially two orders of worship in the early Church that went together to form one basic liturgy. The first part was called the *synaxis*, which simply means 'meeting.' It was patterned after the synagogue worship of the Jews in the years that immediately preceded Christ. It would make sense for the Jewish converts to Christ to retain their basic forms of prayers, hymn singing, Scripture reading, and a homily.

"The second part of the early Christian liturgy was the *Eucharist*, that is 'the thanksgiving.' It's that part of the worship that leads up to and includes the taking of Communion. The form of this service is based upon the liturgy followed by the Old Testament priest in the temple, with the offering no longer that of bulls and goats, but now the body and blood of Christ."

"And that's where the biblical record of First Corinthians 11 comes in?" someone asked.

"Yes—and as a matter of fact, those words of institution were always repeated in Christian worship from the very start," he responded.

"But, Jack, what do you say to the charge that liturgical worship will lead to spiritual death and loss of vitality?" I asked. "I know Churches that are up to here with liturgy, yet seem deader than a doornail."

"I honestly don't know enough yet to answer your question," he replied. "I'm sure we'll get to that matter as we move on in our research. But I can tell you this: Israel was liturgical all through its history, and we have the Old Testament to prove it. Whether they walked with God or not, they were consistently liturgical. And the Church of the New Testament was liturgical from its inception according to the very earliest sources. That's the given. The rest we will have to find out later."

The more we looked through the actual pattern of worship recorded by Justin Martyr, the better we liked it, and the more sense it made. Then it began to dawn on us—even though we called ourselves spontaneous, our spontaneity had itself become a pattern. We had developed our own unique liturgy.

I thought back to our house churches. The same people sat in the same chairs each Sunday morning, the "spontaneous" prayers were basically the same each time; everyone had a set of favorite hymns; the sermon came at the same spot in the service; and we always closed with Communion. In its basic shape, by the way, the *pattern* of what we were doing on Sunday morning was not all that much different from the order that Saint Justin had recorded in A.D. 150.

Next we turned to questions of the Eucharist. "What did you find out about how they viewed the bread and the wine?" we asked. "Did they see it as symbolic or as the actual body and blood of Christ?" (In modern terms: Was it real, or was it Memorex?)

"Actually, it was seen both as symbol and as substance," Jack continued. "But you don't find the term 'transubstantiation' until many centuries later. The key word is *mystery*. The Fathers of the Church saw the consecrated bread and wine as the actual body and blood of Christ, but they never explained the *how*. They confessed it as a blessed mystery."

I was relieved that we were not being pressed into the view of transubstantiation held by the Roman Church, one that I had often criticized as "better living through chemistry." And yet as I thought back to the words of Christ, "This is my body . . . this is my blood," it was apparent that we modern evangelicals had done the words of the Lord a great disservice in the other direction. Besides, you wouldn't have people in first-century Corinth getting sick and dying over mere symbol (I Corinthians 11:17-34). Something serious, something real, had to be taking place as they received the body and blood of the Lord.

It would be unfair to omit the unpleasant side of the story. People did leave us as we began to preach and practice this real or sacramental view of Holy Communion. But this was nothing new. From the Gospel records, we know that the first wave of people to take leave of Christ Himself went away when He taught them, "Unless you eat the flesh of the Son of Man and drink His blood, you have no life in you" (John 6:53). A few lines later, we have verse 66: "From that time many of His disciples went back and walked with Him no more."

From the records of the early Church, it was clear to us that worship was liturgical and that the sacrament of Holy Communion was the centerpiece of the entire service. Honestly, it took some of us, including myself, a while to get emotionally comfortable with liturgy and sacrament. I had become so attached to "winging it." But because of the early and universal witness concerning worship, and its consistency with the New Testament record, we began to teach and experiment with this ancient Christian liturgy in our Churches. And it began, after a while, to seem more like home.

The Church History Report

After a couple of days in preliminary discussion on

worship, we turned next to Jon Braun's study of Church history, picking up immediately after the close of the New Testament.

"The most amazing thing I found in this past three months of reading is the presence of bishops in the first century," he began. "It had been my understanding that bishops came at a later time in the Church, sometime midway through the second century. But here they are, well before A.D. 100.

"You've got Polycarp, a man I had certainly known about. He was Bishop of Smyrna by about A.D. 100. Early writers like Irenaeus tell us he was the spiritual son of the Apostle John, and that he was consecrated bishop by the Apostles themselves.

"Then you've got Clement of Rome, consecrated bishop in that city in A.D. 90, give or take a few years. His connection with the Apostles of Christ is made obvious with his mention by Paul in Philippians 4:3.

"But for me the shocker of them all is Ignatius of Antioch—that's Antioch of Syria, home Church of no less than the Apostles Paul and Barnabas—who was bishop of that city from about A.D. 67 until his martyrdom in 107. Brethren, A.D. 67 is *Bible* times! We're talking about the very heart of the New Testament years. And we know of only two of the Twelve who were dead by that time. Don't you know the other ten would have put up some kind of fierce objection had not the office of bishop been known and approved?"

Bishop Ignatius, of course, is known by all Church historians. He left behind seven letters, written just before his death, to the Churches in the towns he passed through on the way to his martyrdom. They not only spell out with marked clarity the role of the office of bishop, but they tell of the presence of bishops in numerous other Churches as well. He emphatically states that these early bishops were set in office by the Apostles themselves and represent the continuity of the apostolic ministry in the Church.

We had barely recovered from the discovery of liturgy and sacrament in the early Church, and here came bishops! *Early* bishops—as in first century. We began devouring *The Apostolic Fathers*, a collection of the writings of Christians who knew and were taught by the Apostles—including the works of Ignatius, Polycarp, and Clement—and here was a whole new vision of Christendom right before our eyes.

But the New Testament itself was clear regarding bishops, too. *Bishop* is not just a generic term for the function of overseer but also a specific office in the Church. Viewed in that light, the New Testament references to *bishop* became crystal clear.

The earliest New Testament passage comes in Acts 1:20, which deals with the apostasy and replacement of Judas. In the old King James Version it reads, "His bishopric let another take." Some of the newer Protestant translations dodge the word, rendering *bishopric* as "place of leadership" (NIV); "charge" (Moffatt); "position" (Goodspeed); or a bit better, "office" (NASB, NKJV). The fact is, the Greek word in the text is *episcopen*, and the literal meaning is bishopric or episcopate: the office of bishop. By the time the Book of Acts was written, this word no longer meant anything other than bishop. The Twelve, by the way, were universally recognized as the first bishops of the Church.

Then, there is Saint Paul's greeting to the Philippians, written approximately A.D. 65, in which he says, "Paul and Timothy, bondservants of Jesus Christ, to all the saints in Christ Jesus who are in Philippi, with the bishops and deacons" (Philippians 1:1, 2). Taken at face value, this passage shows the office of bishop clearly in place in the Church at Philippi by the middle of the first century.

The question often comes—as it did with us—about the interchangeability of presbyter and bishop in Acts and the Epistles. Aren't there places, like Acts 20 (Paul and the Ephesian elders at Miletus) and Titus 1:5 ("appoint elders in every city") where the terms could refer to either bishop or presbyter? Without question, the possibility of such cross-over does exist in certain passages. By the same token, three specific offices of pastoral service do occur both in the New Testament and in the earliest records of Christian history: bishop, presbyter, and deacon.

For us, the most interesting passage we came across was Acts 15, the Council of Jerusalem. Trouble over keeping Jewish laws had arisen in Antioch, and the Church there, unable to solve the problem locally, referred it to the Apostles and brethren in Jerusalem. The date is A.D. 48 or 49. A council was called to determine God's will and settle the matter. Note what happens. With the presence of the "apostles and the elders" (v. 4) at the meeting, including the Apostle Peter, when everyone had finished speaking, it was James, the brother of the Lord, and not one of the Twelve, who spoke up and said, "Men and brethren, listen to me" (v. 13). And James rendered the final judgment as to what would be done to solve the dispute. Why James? Why not Peter or one of the other Apostles? Because according to all the early writers who address the subject, James was Bishop of Jerusalem by the time that Council was held. And by the record in Acts 15, he certainly functioned accordingly!

A couple of observations have been very helpful personally in my own move from congregational to episcopal church polity. First, just as in the New Testament, any bishop worth his salt in today's world is careful to call for the "amen" of the people. The truth is, a Church headed by a bishop is in reality episcopal, presbyterial, and congregational, all three. The people have a voice, along with the deacons and presbyters. The difference is that in congregational polity, it's one man–one vote, and the sheep usually end up shepherding the shepherd. In episcopal polity, everyone has a voice, but the proverbial buck stops with the bishop. As with James in Acts 15, the bishop makes the final determination.

A second observation is best told by recounting a conversation over breakfast with the president of an evangelical denomination. We had come as far as discovering bishops in the early Church and had committed ourselves to episcopal government. My friend, whose denomination is one of congregational Churches, was somewhat surprised at our shift in direction. He was convinced the New Testament taught only congregational polity.

As the conversation went on, the subject of a new movement among some of his Churches came up. "A lot of our pastors have become enamored with the multiple eldership teaching of men like Ray Stedman," he said. "It's difficult when you're committed to congregational rule, and a more presbyterial emphasis like this comes in. Some of our congregations have already moved in that direction."

"What would you do if the congregation *voted* to go to multiple eldership?" I asked.

"We wouldn't be crazy about it, but we'd go along with it as long as it wasn't permanent," he answered. "That would be presbyterial."

"But what if the people chose as a congregation to make it permanent?" I asked.

"Then I'd have to go in and put a stop to it," he said.

"That would be episcopal," I offered.

In reality, someone always ends up being in charge. We can talk about the rule of the people, egalitarianism, congregationalism, and all the rest, but ultimately one person will march at the head of the column. Doth not nature teach us so? In the Trinity Itself, with three Persons sharing fully the divine nature, the Father is the Fountainhead and the Source of the unity. Be it in heaven or on earth, there are orders of armies, men, and angels.

There is one thing more I wish to say about bishops, a very comforting thing. After years of attempting to live under less leadership, at last I know who is in charge. It is an honor to bend down and kiss the hand of our Archbishop, Philip, with whom I am equal as to our brotherhood in Christ, yet to whom I willingly submit as the hierarch who keeps watch over my soul.

Not many years ago I would have vehemently objected to what I just said: "Well that's fine, but what if you get a bad bishop!" First, Orthodox Christians help select their own bishop. Secondly, each bishop is accountable to a synod of bishops and ultimately to the Patriarch. For that reason when we've had some bad ones, they have been removed. (The heretic Nestorius held the highest office in the Eastern Church, and even he was replaced.) Thirdly, should we select a weak leader, even he is better than no leader at all. Anarchy, be it religious or political, is the worst government of all.

I believe in that old Baptist premise that authority can corrupt, and that absolute authority corrupts absolutely— though no Orthodox bishop has absolute authority. But the opposite is also true: Independence corrupts, and absolute independence corrupts absolutely. For such independence *promotes* absolute authority—absolute authority in the hands of each individual.

There were hierarchs in Israel, hierarchs in the New

Testament, and hierarchs throughout Church history. Biblically, they come with the territory.

The Doctrine Report

We were reeling over liturgy, sacrament, *and* bishops when Richard Ballew brought us his findings on early Church doctrine. We needed a break, and we got one. For as men committed to the Apostles' doctrine, our hearts and minds were both comforted and challenged as we heard how tirelessly the ancient Christians preached and defended our Lord Jesus Christ as fully God and fully man.

"We're going to discover that every major controversy in an Ecumenical Council begins with an all-out attack on Christ Himself," Dick Ballew began. "The first of these came to a head in the summer of A.D. 325, when a Church-wide council was called in Nicea to deal with a heresy called Arianism."

Arius was a presbyter in the Church of Alexandria. He had caused great unrest among the flock by teaching that Jesus Christ was a created being, something less than fully God. His existence began at a point in time, according to Arius. And typical of virtually all false teachers in history, Arius had an arsenal of Bible verses with his own novel interpretations to back him up. He had gained a following among both the clergy and the laity, and his number of devotees was growing. His bishop, the godly Alexander, was deeply concerned and called councils which rejected Arius' view. When the heresy spread, the whole Church and even the emperor became involved.

To address and settle the matter, hundreds of representatives from all over Christendom gathered in Nicea in the memorable summer of A.D. 325 to debate and decide. For Jesus Christ had promised His Church the gift of the Holy

Spirit to lead them into all truth. Here was the first major acid test after the Apostolic era.

As the delegates gathered, including Arius and his followers, another young man came to the fore. Athanasius was a brilliant student of the Scriptures and a devoted follower of Jesus Christ. Seven years earlier at the age of twenty-one, he had already penned a book that was destined to become one of the great Christian classics of all time: *On the Incarnation*. In his introduction to the English translation of this work, C.S. Lewis wrote that when he opened this book, he soon discovered he "was reading a masterpiece" (New York: Macmillan Company, 1946).

At the Council, this admirable young man became one of the chief defenders of the apostolic faith. Arius proved to be no match for the saintly Athanasius. As the weeks of the summer wore on, a strong Orthodox consensus was emerging at Nicea amidst great debate. After three months, a brief document was drafted and presented which contained a summation of Christian teaching on the Person of Jesus Christ. In all, 318 bishops of the Church stepped forward to affirm and to sign what we know today as the first and longest part of the *Nicene Creed*.

The Orthodoxy of Athanasius had prevailed at the Council. Concerning Christ, there never was a time when He was not! That truth became a war cry as the Church would take nearly a century to secure the ground that was gained at Nicea. Arius, though defeated, did not quit. In fact, after Nicea his movement grew. At some points in the years that followed, it appeared that Arianism might prevail—so much so that someone later coined the slogan: "Athanasius against the world."

But ultimately the truth of Christ won out. He who was "begotten of the Father before all time" was preached and worshiped in the one holy Church.

The study of Nicea did several things for us in our journey to Orthodoxy. First and foremost, it gained for us the settled definition of what the New Testament teaches about Jesus Christ. Our preoccupation had been with the work of Christ—*what* He did for us—without the needed concern for *who* He is: the eternal Son of the Father who assumed humanity for our salvation, at once God and man. We had certainly believed in the deity of Christ, but the impact of the incarnation of the Son of God had not hit us with full force. The Nicene Creed became for us, as it always has been for Orthodox Christendom, that doctrinal fence outside of which we dare not wander in our understanding of Christ.

Secondly, Nicea brought to life how councils in the Church are to work: when godly bishops, priests, deacons, and people gather to discern the truth of God, the Holy Spirit will speak to them. The Council of Jerusalem in Acts 15 was not a one-time phenomenon. The whole idea of discerning God's will in consensus made new sense for us.

Thirdly, Nicea introduced us to the other major councils in Church history. For Nicea was the first of the Seven Ecumenical Councils which met between A.D. 325 and A.D. 787, each to confront a Christological error, and each emerging with the truth. These seven councils together complete the foundation of the Church's understanding of the apostolic deposit of the faith and serve as a safeguard of it.

As our week drew to a close, we realized our work had just begun. Had our exercise been merely academic, there would have been little to be concerned with. But our commitment was to change, to adjust. If what we found in our study of the Church was believed and practiced by all Christians everywhere, and if it differed from what we believed and practiced, we would bend. We were tired of novelty and innovation; we yearned for the fullness of the truth.

We left the island to learn to live in liturgy and sacrament and to refocus our lives around the worship of Father, Son, and Holy Spirit. We left understanding and desiring the oversight of bishops and the reality of visible authority in the Church. And we left with a renewed gratitude and love for our Lord Jesus Christ—the Word of God had indeed become flesh and dwelt among us!

4

FINDING THE NEW TESTAMENT CHURCH

B y mid-1975, we had been able to make several decisions concerning the Church from our study of early Christian history.

There was a specific shape or pattern to her worship. It was *liturgical*, coming off the foundation of the worship revealed by God in the Old Testament and fulfilled in Christ, our great High Priest, in the New Testament. Further, and much to our surprise, the post-apostolic writers told us this basic order of worship was essentially the same in the Churches throughout the world.

The early Church was *sacramental*. She confessed with one voice the sacraments (or "mysteries" as they were usually called) as reality, and she practiced them. God gave grace to His people in them. Baptism really *is* for the remission of sins and the giving of the Holy Spirit, exactly as the Apostle Peter had promised his listeners on the day of Pentecost (Acts 2:38). The Eucharistic gifts really *are* the body and blood of Christ as the Lord Himself assured His disciples before His death (Luke 22:19, 20). In the sacrament of marriage, the husband and wife really *do* become one flesh (Ephesians 5:31).

The government or polity of the Church was *hierarchical* from the beginning, a structure which included bishops, presbyters, deacons, and the laity. Our response to that polity was to form the New Covenant Apostolic Order (NCAO) in 1975, hoping to organize something workable yet trying to avoid beginning a new denomination. We were committed to the establishment of Churches bearing these twelve characteristics:

1. Grace
2. True community
3. Vision
4. Authoritative, serving leadership
5. Care
6. Seeing and hearing from God
7. Good works
8. Godliness
9. Orthodox theology
10. Worship
11. The Blessed Hope
12. Catholicity

By early 1979, the NCAO became the Evangelical Orthodox Church. The promise to our people and to each other that we would one day become a part of the historic Church as we found her in our day still remained.

Our understanding of how to discern God's truth and His will for His people was *conciliar*. The early Church addressed the various problems and challenges that faced her in council—be it on the local, regional, or ecumenical level. The sense of the early Christians was to be able to confess together what direction they believed God was giving to the Church.

The very heart of the Apostles' doctrine was the Holy Trinity and the Incarnation of the Son of God. These truths were on the front lines of defense in virtually everything the early Church believed, taught, and fought for.

Let me stress again that, for us, embracing certain of these realities—liturgy, sacrament, episcopal government—did not necessarily come easily. With liturgy and sacrament especially, some of us were "swinging from the floor." That they were true and everywhere in the ancient Church was for us regrettably obvious. We had no argument there. The tough thing about early Christianity for us came in *doing* it.

But isn't that usually the way it is in conversion?

The worship of the Church at the close of its first one thousand years had substantially the same shape from place to place. The doctrine was the same. The whole Church confessed one creed, the same in every place, and she had weathered many attacks. The government of the Church was recognizably one everywhere. And this one Church was Orthodox.

1054: How the West Was Lost

Tensions began to mount in the latter part of the first millennium. They were reaching the breaking point as the second one thousand years began (see the diagram on the next two pages). While various doctrinal, political, economic, and cultural factors were at work to separate the Church in a division that would be the East and the West, two giant issues ultimately emerged above others: (1) should one man, the Pope of Rome, be considered the universal head of the Church? and (2) should the novel phrase *filioque* be added to the Church's creed?

A Time Line of Church History

	New Testament Era		Seven Ecumenical Councils						

ONE HOLY CATHOLIC AND APOSTOLIC CHURCH

33	69	150	325	397	451	589	787	880	988
Pentecost	Bishop Ignatius consecrated in Antioch	Justin Martyr describes liturgy	First Ecumenical Council and the Nicene Creed	Synod of Carthage ratifies biblical canon	Council of Chalcedon	*Filioque* clause added to Nicene Creed by Synod in Spain	Icons approved at Seventh Ecumenical Council	The Photian Schism	Conversion of Russia begins

• 33 Pentecost (A.D. 29 is thought to be more accurate).

• 49 Council at Jerusalem (Acts 15) establishes precedent for addressing Church disputes in Council. James presides as bishop.

• 69 Bishop Ignatius consecrated in Antioch in heart of New Testament era—St. Peter had been the first bishop there. Other early bishops include James, Polycarp, and Clement.

• 95 Book of Revelation written, probably the last of the New Testament books.

•150 St. Justin Martyr describes the liturgical worship of the Church, centered in the Eucharist. Liturgical worship is rooted in both the Old and New Testament.

• 325 The Council of Nicea settles the major heretical challenge to the Christian faith when the heretic Arius asserts Christ was created by the Father. St. Athanasius defends the eternality of the Son of God. The Arians continue their assault on true Christianity for years. Nicea is the first of Seven Ecumenical (Church-wide) Councils.

• 451 Council of Chalcedon affirms apostolic doctrine of two natures in Christ.

• 589 In a synod in Toledo, Spain, the *filioque*, asserting that the Holy Spirit proceeds from the Father *and the Son* is added to the Nicene Creed. This error is later adopted by Rome.

• 787 The era of Ecumenical Councils ends at Nicea, with the Seventh Council bringing the centuries-old use of icons back into the Church.

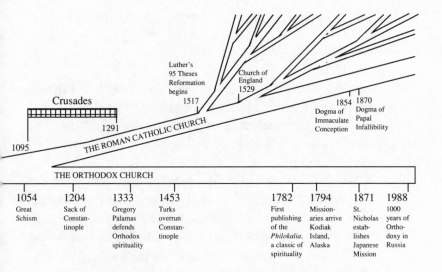

1054	1204	1333	1453		1782	1794	1871	1988
Great Schism	Sack of Constantinople	Gregory Palamas defends Orthodox spirituality	Turks overrun Constantinople		First publishing of the *Philokalia*, a classic of spirituality	Missionaries arrive Kodiak Island, Alaska	St. Nicholas establishes Japanese Mission	1000 years of Orthodoxy in Russia

- 988 Conversion of Russia begins.

- 1054 The Great Schism occurs. Two major issues include Rome's claim to a universal papal supremacy and her addition of the *filioque* clause to the Nicene Creed. The Photian schism (880) further complicated the debate.

- 1095 The Crusades begun by the Roman Church. The Sack of Constantinople by Rome (1204) adds to the estrangement between East and West.

- 1333 St. Gregory Palamas defends the Orthodox practice of hesychast spirituality and the use of the Jesus prayer.

- 1453 Turks overrun Constantinople; Byzantine Empire ends.

- 1517 Martin Luther nails his 95 Theses to the door of the Roman Church in Wittenberg, starting the Protestant Reformation.

- 1529 Church of England begins pulling away from Rome.

- 1794 Missionaries arrive on Kodiak Island in Alaska; Orthodoxy introduced to North America.

- 1854 Rome establishes the Immaculate Conception dogma.

- 1870 Papal Infallibility becomes Roman dogma.

- 1988 One thousand years of Orthodoxy in Russia, as Orthodox Church world-wide maintains fullness of the apostolic faith.

The Papacy

Among the Twelve, Saint Peter was early acknowledged as the leader. He was spokesman for the Twelve before and after Pentecost. He was recorded as the first bishop of Antioch, then later the first bishop of Rome. No one challenged his role.

After the death of the Apostles, as leadership in the Church developed, the bishop of Rome came to be recognized as first in honor, even though all bishops were equal. But after nearly three hundred years, the bishops of Rome slowly began to assume a role of superiority over the others. And without consensus, they ultimately claimed to be the only true successors to Saint Peter.

The vast majority of the other bishops of the Church never questioned Rome's primacy of honor, but they patently rejected the papal claim to be the universal head of the Church on earth. This change from ancient practice was brought about by two factors: the location of four of the five Patriarchs in the East—only Rome was in the West—and the decline of the power of the Roman Empire in the West. The upgraded power of the Roman Pope became one major factor in rending the Roman Church, and all those aligned with it, from the historic Orthodox Church.

The Addition to the Creed

A disagreement about the Holy Spirit also began to develop in the Church. Does the Holy Spirit proceed from the Father? Or, does He proceed from the Father and the Son?

In John 15:26, our Lord Jesus Christ asserted, "But when the Helper comes, whom I shall send to you from the Father, the Spirit of truth who *proceeds from the Father*, He will testify of Me" (emphasis added). This is the basic statement in all of the New Testament about the Holy Spirit "proceeding," and it is clear: He "proceeds from the Father." Period.

Thus when the ancient council at Constantinople in A.D. 381, during the course of its conclave, reaffirmed the Creed of Nicea (A.D. 325), it expanded that Creed to proclaim these familiar words: "And in the Holy Spirit, the Lord and Giver of Life, who proceeds from the Father, who with the Father and the Son is worshiped and glorified."

But some two hundred years later, at a local council in Toledo, Spain (A.D. 589), King Reccared declared that the Holy Spirit should be confessed and taught to proceed from the Father *and the Son*. (The phrase "and the Son" in Latin is the word *filioque;* thus the reference to the problem is often called the "filioque debate.") The King may have meant well, but he was contradicting Jesus' teaching about the Holy Spirit. Unfortunately the local Spanish council agreed with his error, and it gradually spread in the West—though at first it was even rejected by the papacy.

Because of the teaching of the Holy Scriptures as confessed by the entire Church at Nicea and at Constantinople and for centuries beyond, there was no reason to believe anything other than that the Holy Spirit proceeded from the Father.

But centuries later, in a move that to a large extent was motivated by highly intertwined political factors, the Pope of Rome unilaterally changed the universal creed of the Church without an ecumenical council. Though the change was initially rejected in both East and West, even by some of her closest neighboring bishops, Rome managed eventually to get the West to capitulate.

The consequence in the Western Church, of course, has been the tendency to relegate the Holy Spirit to a lesser place than God the Father and God the Son. The change may appear small, but the consequences have proven disastrously immense. This issue, with the Pope departing from the Orthodox doctrine of the Church, became another instrumental cause in perpetuating the separation of the Roman Church from the historic Orthodox Church, the New Testament Church.

The Great Schism

Conflict between the Roman Pope and the East mounted—especially in the Pope's dealings with the Patriarch of Constantinople. It was even asserted that the Pope had the authority to decide who should be the bishop of Constantinople, something which violated historical precedent and which no Orthodox bishop could endure. The net result of this assertion was that the Eastern Church, and in fact the entire Christian Church, was seen by the West to be under the domination of the Pope.

A series of intrigues followed one upon the other as the Roman papacy began asserting an increasing degree of unilateral and often authoritarian control over the rest of the Church. Perhaps the most incredible incident among these political, religious, and even military intrigues, as far as the East was concerned, occurred in the year A.D. 1054. A cardinal, sent by the Pope, slapped a document on the altar of the Church of Holy Wisdom in Constantinople during the Sunday worship, excommunicating the Patriarch of Constantinople from the Church!

Rome, of course, was flagrantly overstepping its bounds by this action. And the repercussions have been staggering. Some not very pretty chapters of Church history were written during the next decades. Ultimately the final consequence of these tragic events was a massive split which occurred between the Roman Catholic Church and the Eastern Church. While some disagree that the West departed from the New Testament Church at this point, the reality remains that the schism was never healed.

As the centuries passed, conflict continued. All attempts at reunion failed, and the split widened. Orthodox Christians agree that in introducing these new doctrines the West had deviated from historic Christianity, and in so doing, set the stage for countless other divisions which were soon to follow.

Our Fork in the Road

So there we were. In our journey through history we had carefully followed over one thousand years of unbroken continuity in the Church.

It goes without saying that we affirmed the Church as found in the pages of the New Testament. We found that same Church in the second and the third centuries, faced with bitter persecution, celebrating her liturgy in homes, caves, and even graveyards; and guided by devoted bishops who often finished the race as martyrs. We found her in the fourth century, defending the faith at Nicea, and in the fifth century at Chalcedon.

We followed her through to the eighth century, studied her great councils, fell in love with her stalwarts, saints, and fathers as they preached the Gospel, warred against the heretics, and reestablished holy imagery in their worship of God. It amazed us how moral and doctrinal corruption in the Church would be boldly faced, and how potential destruction was repeatedly avoided. God was with the Church in the ninth and tenth centuries, in the mission work of Saints Cyril and Methodius, who laid the foundations for the conversion of Russia to Christ which began in A.D. 988.

But then came A.D. 1054, and we were faced with a choice. A split had come. I can still somehow recall the physical *feeling* that I had as I said to my cohorts, "The East is right in resisting papal excesses, and they're right in rejecting the *filioque* clause." And then I drew a deep, new breath. "I guess that makes us . . . Orthodox."

It was at once a feeling of isolation, restlessness, homelessness. Where was this Orthodox Church today? Was it still around? Or had it quietly died away sometime in the late Middle Ages?

The truth is, *none* of us had ever to our knowledge been inside an Orthodox Church. Most of us did not know it existed. For that reason, I am chagrined to report that we decided to try to start it over again!

The West: Reformation and Counter-Reformation

During the centuries following A.D. 1054, the growing distinction between East and West was indelibly marked in history. The East continued in the fullness of New Testament faith, worship, and practice, maintaining the apostolic foundations. Rome headed toward a more rational or scholastic faith. And she became a political superpower in the Western world. The Western or Roman Church also began the Crusades from which would come the deepest and most painful wounds ever inflicted by the West upon the East—and perhaps the most difficult to heal. Then, less than five centuries after Rome committed herself to her course of unilateral action in doctrine and practice, another upheaval was festering—this time not next door in the East but inside the Western gates themselves.

Though many in the West, including some of the popes, had spoken out against many of the growing changes in Roman doctrine and practice, the tide of decline had not been stemmed. Now, a little-known German monk named

Martin Luther inadvertently launched an attack against certain Roman Catholic practices that ended up affecting world history. His famous "Ninety-Five Theses," simply calling for debate on certain issues, were nailed to the church door at Wittenberg in A.D. 1517. In a short time those theses were signaling the start of what came to be called in the West the Protestant Reformation. Luther twice sought an audience with the Pope but was denied, and in A.D. 1521 he was excommunicated from the Roman Church. He had intended no break with Rome, only *reformation* of the Church. Rome's position was not to bend; Luther's was "Here I Stand." The door to unity in the West slammed shut with a resounding crash.

The protests of Luther spread like wildfire fanned by a raging wind. The reforms he sought in Germany were soon accompanied by demands from Ulrich Zwingli in Zurich, John Calvin in Geneva, and hundreds of others all over Western Europe. Fueled by numerous political, social, and economic factors, in addition to religious problems, the Reformation penetrated into virtually every nook and cranny of the Roman Church. Its Western ecclesiastical influence was significantly diminished as this massive division erupted and grew. The ripple effect of that division continues even to our day.

If trouble on the European continent were not enough, the Church of England was in the process of going its own way as well. Henry VIII, amidst his infamous marital problems, replaced the Pope of Rome with himself as head of the Church of England. For only a few short years would the Pope ever again have ascendancy in England. And the English Church herself would come to be shattered by great division that would impact the destiny of the United States and Canada.

As decade followed decade in the West, the many

branches of Protestantism took increasingly diverse forms. There were even divisions which insisted they were neither Protestant nor Roman Catholic. All seemed to share a dislike for the Bishop of Rome and the practice of his Church, and most wanted far less centralized forms of leadership. While some, such as the Lutherans and Anglicans, held on to a basic form of liturgy and sacrament, others, such as the Reformed Churches and the more radical Anabaptists and their descendants, questioned and rejected many biblical realities including hierarchy, sacrament, and historic tradition (no matter when and where they appeared in history), thinking they were freeing themselves of Roman Catholicism.

To this day, many sincere, professing Christians will reject even the biblical data which speaks to the practice of the Christian Church, simply because they think such historic practices are "too Catholic." In its zeal to regain purity, the Protestant movement pursued an agenda of overreaction without even being aware of it.

Thus, while retaining in varying degrees portions of foundational Christianity, neither Protestantism nor Catholicism can lay historic claim to being the fullness of the New Testament Church. In dividing from the Orthodox Church, Rome forfeited its place as the genuine historic expression of the Church of the New Testament. In the divisions of the Reformation, the Protestants—as well-meaning, zealous, and correct as they might have been—failed to return to the New Testament Church.

The Orthodox Church Today

We spent a decade, from 1977 to 1987, getting to know the Orthodox Church—her clergy and her people. It was an incredible experience to find the exact faith in Christ we had come to hold, and to find it embedded securely in a cultural setting we knew almost nothing about. At times we feared we could not possibly relate to the Orthodox Church in the late twentieth century. The highs and the lows, the joys and the disappointments of that decade are chronicled in Part III of this book.

In Part II, "Orthodoxy and the Bible," we will look at specific biblical problems we faced as evangelical Christians who were serious about becoming Orthodox. I will deal with them as clearly, fairly, and honestly as I know how.

As I close Part I, concluding our pilgrimage through the history of Christendom, let me offer a brief word of encouragement. The Church of the New Testament, the Church of Peter and Paul and the Apostles, the Orthodox Church— despite persecution, political oppression, and desertion on certain of its flanks—miraculously carries on today the same faith and life of the Church of the New Testament. Admittedly, the style of Orthodoxy looks complicated to the modern Protestant eye, and understandably so. But given the historical record as to how the Church has progressed, the simple Christ-centered faith of the Apostles is clearly preserved in her practices, services, and even her architecture.

In Orthodoxy today, as in years gone by, the basics of Christian doctrine, worship, and government are never up for renegotiation. One cannot be an Orthodox priest, for example, and reject the divinity of Christ, His virgin birth, Resurrection, Ascension into heaven, or Second Coming. The Church simply has not left her course in nearly two thousand years. She is One, Holy, Catholic, and Apostolic. She is the New Testament Church. The gates of hell have tried repeatedly, but they have not prevailed against her.

Though there are more than 225 million Orthodox Christians in the world today, many Americans are not familiar with the Church. In North America, the Orthodox Church until recently has been largely limited to ethnic boundaries, not spreading much beyond the parishes of the committed immigrants who brought the Church to the shores of this continent. Orthodox Christianity has been, in the words of Metropolitan Philip, "the best-kept secret in America."

PART TWO

ORTHODOXY AND THE BIBLE

5

THE "T" WORD

It's no secret to anyone that a study of Church history immediately bumps one up against one of the great no-no words for most of us from evangelical Protestant backgrounds. To lighten up the discussion a bit, let's call it the "T" word: *Tradition*.

It could be fairly said that there has developed within today's evangelicalism a tradition of being opposed to tradition. And with some good reason. It goes back to the Reformation itself. Much of what men like Luther and Calvin disdained in the Roman Church was that which came under the heading of tradition.

And people like ourselves on a journey to Orthodox Christianity saw the arguments of the Reformation centering quite clearly on the polarity of "the Bible *versus* tradition." It was therefore troubling to us that the word *tradition* was used so very early in Church history. And everyone who wrote of it seemed so *for* it. Our opposition was not to handing things down or passing things on: the literal meaning of the word. It was the idea of incrustation that appeared to us to go along with those things handed down, the man-made inventions and the fear of a traditionalism with the inability to adapt to needed change.

G. K. Chesterton defined tradition as "giving your ancestors a vote." That helped me breathe easier. But the nagging fear remained. What if I get outvoted? I reached for my Bible concordance.

The Two Sides of Tradition

Nobody was tougher on tradition than Jesus Christ. One of the most scathing denouncements in the New Testament was our Lord's condemnation of tradition in Matthew 15:3-9. Look how He so boldly denounced the Pharisees over their appeal to tradition:

> "Why do you also transgress the commandment of God because of your tradition? For God commanded, saying, 'Honor your father and your mother'; and, 'He who curses father or mother, let him be put to death.' But you say, 'Whoever says to his father or mother, "Whatever profit you might have received from me is a gift to God"—then he need not honor his father or mother.' Thus you have made the commandment of God of no effect by your tradition. Hypocrites! Well did Isaiah prophesy about you, saying:
>
> > 'These people draw near to Me
> >   with their mouth,
> > And honor Me with their lips,
> > But their heart is far from Me.
> > And in vain they worship Me,
> > Teaching as doctrines
> >   the commandments of men.' "

This, plus Saint Paul's warning to the Colossians, "Beware lest anyone cheat you through philosophy and empty deceit, according to the tradition of men, according to the basic principles of the world, and not according to Christ" (Colossians 2:8), sum up the strongest biblical exhortations to beware of tradition.

But the New Testament has more to say on the subject. In one of the earliest books in the New Testament, Saint Paul spoke out for tradition. He wrote, "Therefore, brethren, stand fast and hold the traditions which you were taught, whether by word or our epistle" (II Thessalonians 2:15). You can't find a more strongly worded endorsement of tradition than that! Then a few verses later, "But we command you, brethren, in the name of our Lord Jesus Christ, that you withdraw from every brother who walks disorderly and not according to the tradition which he received from us" (II Thessalonians 3:6).

Do we have a contradiction here?

A careful look at the texts tells us that two very different kinds of tradition are being addressed. In the Gospel account and in the Colossians passage we are dealing with the *tradition of men*. In other words, this is tradition that men invent and pass down to others as though it were from God.

Jesus said in the Matthew passage that the tradition of men produced hypocrisy and even vain worship. Saint Paul said man-made tradition would plunder us and take us captive to the world. Such things as the ceremonial washings the Pharisees conducted, which Jesus opposed in Matthew 15, and man-made dietary laws and festivals warned against in Colossians were biblical examples of men's traditions.

And how do we come against such things? Believe it or not, with the other kind of tradition, the tradition of God. It is this kind of tradition which the Apostle Paul commanded that we keep in his second letter to the Thessalonians, quoted a moment ago. Let's take another look.

"Therefore, brethren," he wrote, "stand fast and hold the traditions which you were taught, whether by word or our epistle." Paul was speaking here of the traditions—the things passed on—which the Church received from himself and the other Apostles. This was the "apostles' doctrine" referred to in Acts 2:42. It was that Christ-centered body of truth which Paul and the other Apostles taught and preached.

Note this apostolic tradition took two forms: it came "by word" and by "our epistle." The Scriptures teach us, then, that the holy tradition passed on by the Apostles of Christ included both what they *said*, as they visited the Churches, and what they *wrote*, which we know today as the New Testament. According to the Bible, Scripture itself is a part of holy tradition—the inspired, written part.

The Holy Spirit is the One who brings truth to the Church; He is called the Spirit of Truth. The Twelve were chosen by Jesus Christ to be the foundation-builders of His Church. He promised the Holy Spirit would speak through them. Some of what Christ and His Apostles did and said was recorded in the New Testament, and some was not. Saint Paul tells us to hold fast to both what was taught, and what was written.

You say, "How on earth can we do what these men did and teach what they taught when we weren't there to hear it?" Enter: holy tradition! That which the Apostles and their hand-picked successors planted in the Churches has been passed on through the ages and is still intact today.

You ask, "But how can I trust it?" Let me suggest two reasons that persuaded me to trust it. First, the Lord did say the Holy Spirit would lead His Church into all truth. Either that's true or it isn't. But it is His promise. That does not mean everything any individual Christian has ever said is true. Even Apostles can err. (For example, Paul had to correct Peter for his unwillingness to associate with Gentile Christians, as recorded in Galatians, chapter 2. Saint John, no doubt innocently, twice worshiped angels as noted in the Book of Revelation and was corrected by the angels!) This is precisely why the Church has held councils—to discern and judge under the superintendence of the Holy Spirit what was done and said. Thank God, His promise to lead this Church through her history has been kept—and there have been some trying years.

The second reason I trust the Holy Spirit to lead the Church and preserve her traditions is the way He gave us the Holy Scriptures. Not only were the Scriptures written under the inspiration of the Holy Spirit, the books were *gathered* together under the inspiration of the Spirit.

The Old Testament was written over several centuries by numerous authors, and not compiled in its entirety until much later. The New Testament was written from about A.D. 50 to 95. The notion that the New Testament books just "came together" apart from the decision of the Church is fiction. Though a visible consensus regarding most of the New Testament books existed for years beforehand, it was not until the Synod of Carthage, which met in A.D. 397, that we find the final list of the biblical canon as we know it today.

This is the point. If we can trust the Holy Spirit to guide the Church in discerning the books to be included in the canon of Scripture, then we can trust that He has led the Church in her other decisions as well! And remember—how did the Church know which books were doctrinally sound and thus to be included in the canon? On the basis of the doctrines passed down through holy tradition!

There is no way to take the Scriptures and trash tradition. They come to us as a package. To try to separate the Bible from tradition is to divide the work of the Holy Spirit into approved and disapproved categories—and that sails dangerously close to the winds of unforgivable sin.

Late Traditions

One of the groans which we uttered in the course of our journey was over the matter of late traditions. We knew that up until the eleventh century the Church was one. Until that time, Christians looked to the great Ecumenical Councils as the guideposts for the interpretation of Scripture and for the formulation of what was to be believed.

But with the departure of Rome from Orthodox Christianity, something dramatic changed. Because she was no longer accountable to the whole of the historic Church, Rome was now free to teach the universality of the Pope and the altered Nicene Creed with the novel *filioque* clause. She was likewise on her own to introduce other new dogmas and practices as well. And introduce them she did—and likely she will again.

The Protestant Reformers were not reacting against a "straw man" when they attacked such innovations as a burning purgatory, the universal authority of the pope, and indulgences. These were all three late additions to the faith, with no roots at all in apostolic tradition.

For example, in 1854 Rome established the dogma of the immaculate conception of the Virgin Mary. According to this teaching, not only was Christ born on earth without sin, but Mary entered the world without original sin. Many ask then, why not back up to her parents, their parents, and on through the countless genealogies all the way back to Eden?

In 1870, scarcely more than a century ago, Rome added yet another dogma to her growing collection of new traditions. This time, it was the Pope again. Now he was not only universal, he was infallible.

No wonder Protestants are scared to death of tradition!

It's a hard saying. My Roman Catholic friends don't like it when I say it, but I'm saying it anyway. Rome stepped away from apostolic tradition in 1054. She left one thousand years of unity in the Church behind. No, she's not all wrong—not for a moment. But she is saddled with a collection of dogmas that simply do not square with holy tradition. And my opinion is that she is moving further away from Orthodox Christianity, not closer. A growing proportion of her priests, nuns, and laity seem to possess a spirit of rebellion and even anarchy—liberation theology in South America, feminism and theological liberalism in North America, and in Europe the gamut goes from no-show apathy to brittle arch-conservatism.

It's time for Rome to come back home to the unity of the Church and the faith of the Apostles and holy Fathers which she once held so dear. It's time to come back to the fullness of holy tradition!

Saddled even more with late tradition is the Protestant movement. Whereas Rome generally has added to the faith, Protestantism has subtracted from it. In an effort to shake off Roman excesses, modern Protestants have sorely over-corrected their course. The reductionism that results cripples Protestant Christians in their quest for full maturity in Christ and in steering a steady course in doctrine and worship.

Mary has become a no-name; holy communion, a quarterly memorial; authority and discipline in the Church, a memory; doctrine, a matter of personal interpretation, constantly up for renegotiation. Name one established Protestant denomination that has held on fully to the faith of even its own founders—to say nothing of its adherence to the apostolic faith.

Finding the Family

We were searching for our spiritual family. And many of the emotions we felt and situations we encountered were similar to those of adopted children looking for their biological parents.

We have some good friends in Santa Barbara, let's call them Don and Polly Browner. Polly is adopted. When she was born in 1948, her mother was separated from her father and could not afford to keep her and raise her. So even before the day of her birth arrived, arrangements were made for the baby to be adopted by an eager Christian family who had one daughter but were unable to have more children.

Polly learned she was adopted when she was four years old. She was playing one day, when for no apparent reason she asked, "Mommy, are you my real mommy?" Taken off guard, her mother told her that she was not, but that she couldn't love her any more if she were.

From that time on, Polly began a secret search. And it was intensive. At the age of thirteen, she became obsessed with her adoption. It wasn't because she was unhappy or thought her parents weren't doing a good job raising her; she became preoccupied with the idea that somewhere in this world there were people who were related to her and who might look like her.

A short time later, Polly was rummaging through her father's file box and found her adoption papers. She skimmed through the documents and at the bottom found the signatures of her two natural parents. The last name was easy to remember—too easy, for who knows how many

Americans share that same last name: *Smith*. Polly's desire to find her natural parents grew even more dramatically during her teenage years.

Whenever she walked outside, she looked at faces—faces she hoped would look like hers. And if she found anyone she thought resembled her, she stopped the person and asked questions. If she was in a strange town, she looked up *Smith* in phone books.

In 1968, Polly met Don who eventually would be her husband. Don became as interested in solving the mystery as Polly. On their first date, they visited the Hall of Records in Los Angeles, the city where she was born. But she discovered that her records were stored and sealed in Sacramento. They stopped by the hospital that had delivered her into the world but found nothing.

In mid-December, 1975, knowing that at one time her natural father had held a California driver's license, she and Don ran his name through the Department of Motor Vehicles' computer. The data that surfaced gave them an address in a small California town. They headed for the nearest pay phone, but they discovered no one with her father's first name under Smith. After about two days of studying the data, they figured out Polly's father had financed a car through the Bank of America.

Now, an entire paper chase episode was opening up. The bank told Polly that Mr. Smith had indeed taken out a loan but had since moved to a large Midwestern city. A call to information in that city yielded no listing. However, the tax assessor's office in the same city indicated a family by the name of Walker had bought a home from Mr. Smith, Polly's father, a year earlier. And the assessor just happened to have Mrs. Walker's phone number. By now it was New Year's Eve afternoon, 1975.

Bright and early New Year's day, when the Browners

thought it was late enough in the Midwest, they called Mrs. Walker. Don, now Polly's husband, did the talking. When Don asked her if she knew Mr. Smith, she said indeed she did—he was her nephew! Don began asking questions, so many in fact that he finally had to tell her why he was calling. In response, she said she knew the Smiths had had three children but didn't know anything about a fourth. That was the first Polly learned she had a brother and two sisters.

Finally, Mrs. Walker suggested that Don call Polly's father's sister, who also lived in town, to get further information. She volunteered Polly's aunt's number.

Polly's aunt was very evasive. She didn't believe a word Don was saying, and would not tell them where Polly's father was or anything about him. Don pleaded but she hung up. Polly was up against a brick wall again.

Two hours went by. Polly finally convinced Don to let her call the aunt. Even after Polly repeated the whole story, her aunt was still suspicious. Finally Polly asked her aunt to at least relay the information to her father and to let him be the judge as to whether he wanted to get in touch.

About an hour and a half later, the phone rang. It was a collect call from Mr. Smith. Polly swallowed hard and accepted the call. During the forty-five minute conversation, Polly found out that after her adoption, her mother and her dad had gotten back together for a time and had had two more children. Her mother had been living alone in Southern California for the past ten years.

Later, the phone rang again. It was her natural sister, Betty. They talked about twenty-five minutes. Polly couldn't get over how much they sounded alike.

Twenty minutes passed, and the phone rang a third time. It was Polly's natural mother. By the end of that conversation, Polly was a basket case! But, even though drained emotionally, she was ecstatic. Two days later the first pictures arrived. There were resemblances, but none of them looked even vaguely like she thought they might.

Happy New Year, 1976!

In the weeks and months that followed, Polly was able to personally meet her natural parents, her brother and her sisters. She had found her natural family.

If you are anything like me, or anything like Polly Browner, you, too, are on a search for your spiritual family. Oh, it won't be the first-century Church when you find her, because here we are on the doorstep of the twenty-first century. Now, as we say, she's a little older and perhaps even a little wiser. But she's the same Church. For she has kept the traditions of her Founder and His Apostles intact.

Family Tradition

What is our holy tradition? It is the "one Lord, one faith, one baptism; one God and Father of all" (Ephesians 4:5, 6). It is that precious faith, "once for all delivered to the saints" (Jude 3). It is Orthodox Christianity.

At this point you might be saying, "Okay—I understand there's good tradition and bad tradition, the tradition of God and the tradition of men. But rather than using the 'T' word, why can't we just say we believe the Bible?"

We can. We do. But we must say more. Why? Because the Jehovah's Witness at your door also carries a Bible and says he believes it. Tradition is there not just to preserve the Bible but to interpret it. Without the Church there to interpret, to shed the light of holy tradition on those chapters and verses, you and the Jehovah's Witness are in a dead heat: his interpretation versus yours.

The Church is thus our guardian of the truth. In the

words of Saint Paul himself, she is "the pillar and ground of the truth" (I Timothy 3:15).

Let's say you're driving down the street going fifty in a thirty-five mile per hour zone. The city statutes have designated thirty-five as the maximum speed on city streets. But who is it that pulls you over, the book of city statutes? No, it's a traffic officer. For the same civil laws that set the speed limit also provide the city with a police force. The officer is there to enforce the laws and statutes.

So it is with the Bible, the Church, and tradition. The Scriptures are true—holy, just, and good. But they were never meant to stand alone. Their enforcer and interpreter—indeed, their writer—is the Church. The Church is also the doer of the Word. And the way things are done and have been done is preserved for us in holy tradition. But even the Church did not originate her tradition.

The tradition has one source: God Himself. To begin with, the Apostles received it from Jesus Christ and passed it on unchanged and undiminished to the Churches which they formed. Jesus had told the Twelve that they still had truth to learn, that the Holy Spirit would lead them into it.

On the Day of Pentecost, God's Old Covenant people became His New Covenant people as they were baptized into Christ. As the Church developed, guided by the Spirit, the people brought with them their worship, given to them hundreds of years earlier, patterned after things in heaven (see Hebrews 9:23) but now centered in Christ Himself. The tradition of Christian worship was born as the old gave way to the new.

And with the help of the Holy Spirit, the Church learned early on to be self-correcting. If error crept in, the Apostles moved at once to put things back in order—sometimes through personal visits, sometimes through letters, sometimes by both. This itself became tradition, and the letters, inspired by the Holy Spirit, were read, reread, copied, and passed on. We know them today as the New Testament Epistles.

About the same time, the Holy Spirit prompted Matthew, Mark, Luke, and John to set down in writing for the Church the Gospel of Jesus Christ. What they wrote matched what they preached, for the source was the same. The written word was received by the people who had believed the spoken word. For it was all one message, one body of truth, one tradition. They took care to pass it on to faithful men, who in turn would teach others also.

Thus, out of the Church and under the guidance of the Holy Spirit came the Bible—the absolutely unique part of her tradition—which she carefully guarded, interpreted, defended, and preached. But also out of the Church and guided by the same Holy Spirit came the Apostolic traditions not recorded in the Scripture, but consistent with Scripture—to which the Scripture tells us to adhere.

I was speaking not long ago to a group of students at a large, independent Protestant seminary, which is known for its firm stand on the inspiration of the Bible but holds to numerous doctrinal tenets foreign even to the rest of Protestantism. It seemed they were so intent on safeguarding the inspiration of Scripture that they had ignored the interpretation of Scripture and had fallen prey to their novel dogmas. They had sidestepped, even despised, holy tradition.

Finally I said, "Look, you brothers have the right Bible. No argument there. And you serve the right Savior. Jesus Christ is our Lord. What you need is the right Church, that family of undivided Christendom which has preserved the faith and worship of the Apostles and their followers."

It is to this Orthodox Church, which has paid with her

lifeblood for twenty centuries to keep safe her holy tradition, that we have finally come. It took a decade to find her, but thank God, she is still here to be found. Within her walls are the treasures of the apostolic faith, safely preserved throughout the centuries by the Holy Spirit who lives within her and gives her new life.

6

WHY WE WORSHIP THE WAY WE DO

I t was one of those late-night, early-mornings when I woke up and could not go back to sleep. Usually I would either watch Charlie Rose on Channel 12 or get up and read the Bible. I had been pondering something or other in the Book of Acts, so on this particular night I chose to read the Bible.

When I do specific Bible study or prepare for sermons, I use the *New King James Version* (NKJV) as my text. But for times like these late night sessions, I'll usually select another version for a fresh look at a familiar passage. On this night, I chose the *New American Bible* (NAB), a somewhat chatty and engaging translation done under the auspices of the Roman Catholic Church.

Liturgical Worship in Scripture

I was moving through Acts and got to chapter 13, which opens with the Church in Antioch when they were sending out Paul and Barnabas. And then I came to verse two: "On one occasion, while they were engaged in the liturgy of the Lord and were fasting, the Holy Spirit spoke to them" (NAB). *Hold it!* I thought to myself. *Everybody knows the text says that they were "ministering to the Lord and fasting." There can't be liturgy as early as Acts 13.*

So I grabbed my Greek New Testament from the bookshelf next to my desk. Right there, in Acts 13:2, for all to see: *leitourgounton* was the Greek word. You don't even need to know Greek to figure out the meaning! There is liturgy in Acts 13. It was the Protestants who had altered the translation.

According to the New Testament, we've got Christian liturgy in Antioch, Paul's home Church, before A.D. 50. So much for the theory that liturgy was what crept into the Church when people forgot to rely on the Holy Spirit for spontaneity in worship. In fact, here in Acts 13:2 you not only have a liturgical setting for worship, but you have the Holy Spirit speaking to the Church *during* the liturgy! I thought about my homilies of the past. Many would need to be retooled before the next time out of the mothballs.

This passage gives great hope to those of us who wrestle with the fear of "dead liturgy." In reality, there is no such thing as liturgy being dead. Liturgy is either true or false. It's people who are dead or alive. I'll tell you my dream of Orthodox Christianity at its best: live, spiritual people worshiping God in true liturgy! There's no match for it. And that is precisely what Jesus envisioned when He told the woman at the well that the Father was looking for people who would worship Him "in spirit and truth" (John 4:24).

That night started me off on a whole new study of worship in the Bible. By this point in our journey, it was no secret to me or to any of my colleagues that all the early records—the *Didache*, Justin Martyr, Hippolytus—talked about the Church from the New Testament as being liturgical in her worship. But now the verb form of the old Greek noun *leitourgia* was showing up in the New Testament itself. What were the roots of this phenomenon?

My mind jumped ahead to the place in Hebrews where it says that God told His people in the Old Testament to worship according to His directives in ways patterned after things in heaven (Hebrews 8:5 and 9:23). In other words, Israel didn't worship just any way she pleased. God told her how, and it was done that way, so that it would participate with what was done in heaven.

A Vision of Worship in Heaven

That triggered the next question: How *was* worship done in heaven? The first passage to come to mind was Revelation 4, where the Apostle John sees heavenly worship in his vision of the emerald throne, the twenty-four elders in vestments of white and crowns of gold, the seven flaming candles, and all the rest. "Doesn't seem much like Protestant evangelicalism," I muttered quietly to myself. "But there must be somewhere earlier, like in the Old Testament, where there's a record of somebody seeing heaven, like Ezekiel or Elijah or Isaiah. That's it! Isaiah. Isaiah, chapter 6. If the Old Testament liturgy was patterned after heavenly worship, Isaiah 6 certainly qualifies as a prototype."

For me, the easiest way to lay hold of the message of Isaiah 6 was to underscore the sensory verbs, and that is how I will pass it on to you. The event took place in "the year that King Uzziah died," about 700 B.C. Isaiah's description was remarkably detailed as to exactly what it was that he experienced. And what he recorded was not only understandably similar to worship in the tabernacle of old, it was incredibly like the historic worship of the Christian Church! Take an extra moment or two and read Isaiah's brief account of his visit to heaven slowly and thoughtfully.

In the year that King Uzziah died, I saw the Lord sitting on a throne, high and lifted up, and the train of His robe filled the temple. Above it stood seraphim; each one had six wings: with two he covered his face, with two he covered his feet, and with two he flew. And one cried to another and said:

"Holy, holy, holy is the LORD of hosts;
 The whole earth is full of His glory!"

And the posts of the door were shaken by the voice of him who cried out, and the house was filled with smoke. So I said:

"Woe is me, for I am undone!
 Because I am a man of unclean lips,
 And I dwell in the midst of a people
  of unclean lips;
 For my eyes have seen the King,
 The LORD of hosts."

Then one of the seraphim flew to me, having in his hand a live coal which he had taken with the tongs from the altar. And he touched my mouth with it, and said:

"Behold, this has touched your lips;
 Your iniquity is taken away,
 And your sin purged."

Also, I heard the voice of the Lord, saying:

"Whom shall I send, and who will go for Us?"

Then I said, "Here am I! Send me" (Isaiah 6:1-8).

How would you like worship on Sunday to be that powerful? The fact is, you can come close! Let us look at the elements, the details, of Isaiah's eyewitness account of heaven's liturgy and see how it impacted him specifically via his five senses and his understanding of mission.

Worship as Seeing

Isaiah saw something. To begin with, he saw the Lord high and lifted up with the train of His robe filling the temple. "The Lord" in this passage was the eternal Son of God. The Apostle John in his Gospel was quoting Isaiah's prophecies concerning Christ and was referring to Isaiah's vision of heaven when he wrote: "These things Isaiah said when he saw His glory and spoke of Him" (John 12:41).

Let me ask: Have you ever wished you could see Jesus Christ? I mean, see Him as you would see other people? I recall going through a special stage as a child, and then later as a young adult, where I thought having faith would be so much easier if I could, just for once, *see* the Lord.

Ultimately the faithful will see Him, face to face. And we are called to walk by faith and not by sight. But Isaiah got to see Him, and so did all the people in the Gospels who knew Him, and so did Stephen and Paul and John, who got to see Him even after the Ascension. So how about people like you and me?

Clearly, the Church from antiquity has provided her people a means of seeing the Lord, visual aids if you will. In his classic book, *The Shape of the Liturgy*, Dom Gregory Dix tells how in the primitive house-churches in Rome when believers gathered for worship, the grim old pictures of ancestors were taken down from the walls. They were "replaced by mosaics of Old Testament worthies and the Christian saints" (p. 27).

Then, when the persecutions died down, and church buildings were no longer just homes of volunteers but permanent, symbols and images became more bold. Behind the altar in almost every Church there came to be, according to Dix, a "representation concentrated on the figure of the Son, who is 'the express image' of the Father" (p. 32). In the Churches of the East it was the image or icon of Christ Pantocrator, or Ruler over all. In the West, it was Christ as the Lamb of God, our Redeemer.

So you did see Christ in worship. Rather than set before her people a mere blank wall or wood panel or floral display, the Church in her wisdom has historically displayed the icons of the Lord Jesus Christ and His heroic saints. These images, these windows to heaven, provide for those who worship Him the opportunity to see, with the eyes of faith, through the medium of paint and canvas, to the Original.

The objection sometimes comes, "But does not the Second Commandment in Exodus 20 forbid imagery?" It forbids false images—idols—but not imagery as such. For if proper imagery were forbidden, why, just six chapters later in Exodus 26:1, would God command, "Moreover you shall make the tabernacle with ten curtains of fine woven linen, and blue, purple, and scarlet thread; with artistic designs of cherubim you shall weave them"?

Thomas Howard has said that the Divine Liturgy is the grandest multi-media event of all time. And it's even more than multi-media, for we *participate* in it. We experience worship with all five senses, plus the sense of faith. According to Dorothy Sayers we have no way to think, except in pictures. It's time we capture our imaginations for Christ again, and historically the Church has done this through the use of icons in her worship.

Isaiah saw more than the Son of God, however. There was a throne, there were seraphim, there were doors in the heavenly sanctuary. And there was an altar.

Frankly, I had for years dismissed altars as "old covenant" and unnecessary because of the once for all sacrifice of Christ. But again, the entire ancient Church had them. Did early Christians know something we do not? Often, when the place of worship was in the catacombs, the tomb of a departed brother or sister in Christ would serve as the altar. In the house churches, the altar was generally in the place which during the week would be the dining room.

The Book of Hebrews says plainly: "We have an altar" (Hebrews 13:10). Certainly the sacrifice of Christ is complete; we can add nothing to it. For the early Christians the altar represented the Cross. No longer was it the altar of sacrifice for the blood of bulls and goats, but now it was the reality of the Cross of Christ, where He gave for us eternally His broken body and shed blood. And so it is to this day. It is from His holy altar that we are given to receive His sacred Gifts: His body and blood in the great Thanksgiving feast!

Worship as Hearing

On this day in heaven, Isaiah saw but he also heard. The hymn he heard the angels sing, "Holy, holy, holy is the LORD of hosts," became the biblical basis for the thrice-holy hymn known as the *Sanctus* in the West and the *Trisagion* in the East. It has been sung on the earth for centuries just as it has been sung in heaven presumably from all eternity.

When I was small, Guy Lombardo was one of the great swing band leaders in America. His slogan was as famous as he was: "The Sweetest Music This Side of Heaven." I do not presume to know Lombardo's religious convictions, but it is certainly safe to say that in the world of his day, somehow people knew that the ultimate in music had to come from heaven. And heaven's music is what Isaiah heard.

While we perhaps may justify earthly choirs from the singers in the temple, we can clearly substantiate angelic ones in heaven. The angelic chorus becomes the basis for our choirs in worship. They are not there to replace the singing of the people but to buttress it with the highest level of choral beauty. And so, as the priest moves through the doors and out among the worshipers carrying the soon-to-be-consecrated bread and wine in what is called the Great Entrance, the choir sings:

> Let us who mystically represent the cherubim
> And sing to the life-giving Trinity
> The thrice-holy hymn,
> Let us now lay aside all earthly cares
> > that we may receive the King of all,
> Who comes invisibly upborne by the angelic hosts.
> Alleluia! Alleluia! Alleluia!

One of the things that has comforted me most in the worship of God through the time-proven liturgy of the Church is that so many of the passages of the Bible that I never underlined have come to life. It is as though heaven's drama of worship is playing live, right in my home town and in the very Christian community to which I belong. Since the liturgy is a procession of the people of God to His heavenly throne, not only is Christ really present with us, we are really present with Him, as the Scriptures say, "in the heavenlies."

Truth is, there is just one Divine Liturgy, one Holy Communion, in *all* the universe—the one in heaven. We who gather as the Church here on earth are called to join in and participate with heaven's hosts. And to do so, we take great pains in our worship to make it consistent—and not to clash—with the worship before the throne of God. Or, to use the words of the Lord's Prayer, we want to be sure that in our worship we are carrying out God's will "on earth as it is in heaven."

Why have most modern Protestant bodies—traditional, evangelical, and charismatic—left this historic shape of Christian worship? To answer, let me coin a word, *Romophobia*. How many times have you heard people resist liturgy with the excuse, "It's too Catholic"? Well, *so what!* Is the issue whether or not Rome does it? It's time we *all* come back to the Bible. And the Bible teaches that worship is liturgical—both in heaven and on earth.

My friend, an Orthodox priest, had never in his life been to a service in an evangelical Church. Since he was busy on Sunday mornings, he decided to visit a local evangelical Church one Sunday evening. "How did you respond?" I asked him. "What did you think?"

"Well, the preaching was really good," he answered. "The pastor stayed carefully with the text, and I felt he communicated the Gospel quite clearly. I was impressed."

He paused for a moment, trying to put the rest of his reactions into words. After a couple of false starts, he finally blurted out, "But the rest of the service was like . . . well, I guess you could call it a Christian Lawrence Welk Show."

He went on to describe all the special musical numbers, the choral arrangements, and the words to those songs that centered on the *me* whose needs are met, rather than on our Triune God before whom we bow in worship. We have lost true worship in modern Christianity, and we must by the grace of God get it back!

Worship as Touch and Taste

"And he touched my mouth with it," Isaiah said of the seraph who brought him the coal from off the altar. He had seen something, heard something, and now the prophet *felt* something. A burning coal had been taken from heaven's altar with tongs and carried by the seraph to meet Isaiah's lips. What is the meaning of this act?

After Isaiah had seen the Lord and heard the hymn of the angels crying holiness to Him, the prophet gave a most predictable response, "Woe is me, for I am undone." It was what a child psychologist called on a recent TV program "the Oh-oh Feeling," which he described as the emotion of a child when he is caught red-handed in an act of disobedience.

You and I would have felt the same as Isaiah did. Here he was, a citizen of Israel at a time when God was greatly disappointed with His chosen nation because of their disobedience and lack of faith. We read just one chapter earlier in Isaiah 5 that God had looked for good grapes in His vineyard and gotten wild ones. "I will lay it waste," He warned in verse six. Isaiah knew he was part of all this.

Now, all of a sudden, he found himself swept up to heaven facing the Lord of Glory! His train filled the temple. The angels were singing, so much so that the doorposts shook. Look at Isaiah's response:

> "Woe is me, for I am undone!
> Because I am a man of unclean lips,
> And I dwell in the midst of a people of unclean lips;
> For my eyes have seen the King,
> The LORD of hosts" (Isaiah 6:5).

He was standing before the mighty Son of God, confessing the uncleanness of his own lips and that he lived in the midst of unclean people. What brought this conviction of sin? "My eyes have seen the King." When any of us really see Christ, we come unglued or *undone* to use the Bible word, because then we see our sin most vividly. It's the "Oh-oh Feeling" raised to the highest power.

So then what happened? The same thing that always happens when our sins are laid before the Son of God. The angel took the coal, the symbol of the sacrament, off the altar, touched the lips of Isaiah with it and proclaimed for all of heaven to hear: "Behold, this has touched your lips; your iniquity is taken away, and your sin is purged."

Isn't that just like the Son of God, to not only take away sin but to purge or separate it from us, as we read in another place, "as far as the east is from the west" (Psalm 103:12)? "Jesus Christ is the same yesterday, today, and forever" (Hebrews 13:8). He will do the same for us as we confess our sins and receive His gift today from off the altar. Can you see how the coal teaches us the power of the sacrament? This is why, from centuries ago until this day, when a priest of the Orthodox Church receives the body and blood of Christ at the altar, his confession is precisely that of godly Isaiah as he repeats, "Behold this has touched my lips, my iniquity is taken away and my sins are purged!"

We who have lived apart from the worship and the sacrament of Christ need His holy touch. You may go to this Church or that, seek the teaching of this preacher or that, this spiritual experience or that, but the truth is you will never find real worship, heavenly worship, anywhere—*anywhere*—apart from the life-giving grace of Christ at His holy Eucharist. I, and thousands of others, know. We tried. And we consistently came up short.

The psalmist said, "Taste and see that the LORD is good;

Blessed is the man who trusts in Him" (Psalm 34:8). At His Holy Table, it is given us to taste, see, and touch. Isaiah was touched by the flaming coal of God's forgiveness, tasting personally His goodness. And from the altar of God comes that very same provision for us and for our sins to this day. Let us come boldly therefore, with faith and love, and draw near to His throne of mercy.

Worship as Smell

When Isaiah came to the heavenly temple, another of his senses went to work. He smelled something for "the house was filled with smoke."

I recall as vividly as if it had taken place yesterday walking into the sanctuary of Saint Innocent Orthodox Church, Tarzana, California, and experiencing for the first time the lingering fragrance of incense used a few hours earlier in a morning service. I was offended. "I'll buy Orthodox doctrine," I said to myself (I already had bought it), "but they'll never catch me using incense."

A couple of months later I was back at Saint Innocent for a worship service and, naturally, I reexperienced the odor of incense. This time it was rather pleasant because it brought back memories of liking other things about my previous visit.

That next week I began to think my way back through the Scriptures. Israel used incense in her worship. We read repeatedly of the altar of incense with the rising smoke signifying the prayers of the saints. Isaiah in his heavenly vision of Christ and His angelic hosts saw the Lord high and lifted up "and the house was filled with smoke" (Isaiah 6:4). Incense was one of the three gifts brought to the infant Jesus by the wise men. Revelation 8 tells us of incense in the eternal heavens. *Why not now?* I recall thinking to myself, realizing that it was generally modern Protestants who were the exception, not the rule. The rest of Christendom has used incense in worship for two thousand years!

But then the thought came, *Is it all that big a deal? Should we make incense an issue? Is it worth pressing for?*

Some years ago, I was planning a trip to Minneapolis to move my wife's mother, Olga Grinder, to the West Coast to live near us in Santa Barbara. She was seventy-nine, and family consensus—including hers—was that she did not need another Minnesota winter, especially living by herself. I would go back, help her pack, put the house up for sale, and accompany her back West.

Peter Jon, my youngest of six, who was then eleven, asked to go along. "P.J., you're right in the middle of the school year," Marilyn reasoned. "Besides, it's a pretty expensive trip."

"I can make up the schoolwork—I'll even take homework assignments along," P.J. rejoined, "And I'll help buy my ticket from my savings account."

We were both unconvinced and shook our heads "no" until the next sentence, the corker. "Dad, Mom, all the other kids were older the last time we visited Grandma. They remember, and I don't. She'll sell the house, and I'll go through life and not remember what Grandma's house was like."

I phoned the travel agent the following morning to reserve two seats instead of one.

It was the end of October when we journeyed to Grandma's. We were right at the end of the colorful fall season. Our first night there, we were sitting together, the three of us, in the den, eating take-out Chinese food. P.J. was on the couch with a TV tray in front of him. "Do you remember anything about Grandma's house?" I asked.

"Yeah, two things," he answered immediately as

though he were prepared for the question. "I remember the den wallpaper. The last time I was here the little girl across the alley pushed me off her swing, and I cut my knee. Grandpa brought me in and laid me here on the couch, and I remember looking at this wallpaper all afternoon."

"What's the other thing?" I asked.

"The smell," he said. Then he giggled at what he had heard himself say. "I don't want to be weird, but Grandmas' houses always smell a certain way."

Olga and I both blinked back the tears.

Of course Grandmas' houses all have a certain smell. And so do God's houses. The tabernacle had a smell, the temple had a smell, heaven has a smell, and the Church has a smell. It's the smell of incense, and it involves our sense of smell in worship.

Personally, I find that incense helps me keep my mind from wandering during worship. And now, the minute I walk inside the Church, my sense of smell notifies my brain of what I am there to do: bow down to Father, Son, and Holy Spirit and pray. Is incense worth scrapping for?

Let the prophet Malachi give God's answer to that question:

> "For from the rising of the sun,
>   even to its going down,
> My name shall be great among
>   the Gentiles;
> In every place incense shall be
>   offered to My name,
> And a pure offering;
> For My name shall be great
>   among the nations,"
> Says the LORD of hosts (Malachi 1:11).

The Scriptures tell us that as the Gospel would spread to the Gentile world, in the age of the Church, incense would be offered in every place. Incense is prophesied to accompany the worship of the Christian Church. That settles it for me! When something God reveals is missing in our worship, I believe in getting busy to restore it.

Worship as Mission

There was a final step in the events of the day Isaiah saw, heard, tasted, touched, and smelled the worship of heaven. That was, he did something. When his sins had been purged, Isaiah was questioned by the Lord. Given the discouraging state of affairs in Israel, God was looking for a prophetic spokesman to call them back to center. "Whom shall I send, and who will go for Us?" (the "Us" there being a wonderful Old Testament reference to the Holy Trinity).

Isaiah replied without delay, "Here am I! Send me."

We're not all called to be prophets of God ("all are not prophets, are they?"—I Corinthians 12:29), and surely the liturgy, though heavenly, is rarely as dramatic as this. But this is sure: All of us who worship God are called to freely and firmly say yes to Jesus Christ in whatever He asks us to do.

This is why in the Divine Liturgy at the end of several litanies, the priest or deacon leads us in saying, "Let us commit ourselves, each other, and all our lives unto Christ our God." How much of ourselves do we give over to the Lord? Everything—*all* our lives. That is our yes to Him.

In the Orthodox Church, there is each week an altar call: to partake of the body and blood of Christ. There is an invitation hymn: "Receive me today, O Son of God!" And we are asked to make a commitment to Christ. Let us never leave the liturgy, therefore, without laying down our lives afresh to Him, to be His servants, His ambassadors, in the world to which we go.

7

CALL NO MAN FATHER

Several decades have passed since Bing Crosby donned clerical garb and portrayed a role on the silver screen for which he would be endeared even to this day—Father O'Malley. At our house, over the years, Marilyn and I grab the kids and stay up late to watch the Christmas reruns on T.V.

Somewhat earlier in the century, one of the great humanitarians of our time, Father Flanagan, founded Boys' Town in Nebraska. The home became a nationally-known refuge for homeless young men. In many ways, Mother Teresa of India is his contemporary female counterpart, caring for the poor and downtrodden of her land.

But what are we to make of these titles? We admire the work and character of these people, but does not the Bible issue the command to call no man father?

In my more radical Protestant days I would only call a priest *father* if I absolutely had to—sometimes offering a silent prayer for the Lord to forgive me. And now that I'm a priest, I see the same hesitancy in others. It was one of the issues we struggled with as we made our way to Orthodoxy.

Certain statements made by Jesus have often been the basis of great controversy, both inside and outside the Church. His saying in Matthew 23:9, "Do not call anyone on earth your father; for One is your Father, He who is in heaven," has proven to be no exception. I must confess it was a major issue for us as evangelical Christians to call the pastors of Orthodox parishes father.

At Issue Is Interpretation

Some interpreters inside Protestantism are sure Jesus was warning against addressing church leaders as father. They, of course, are interpreting "father" in this Scripture to mean spiritual father. Therefore, they refuse to call their clergymen father, preferring instead such titles as *pastor, reverend,* or perhaps even *brother.*

At the outset, therefore, let me point out that "spiritual father" is an interpretation of the Lord's statement rather than what He actually said. Mind you, I am not denying the need for interpretation of Scripture. Instead, I am pointing out that the Lord said "father," not "spiritual father."

What is at issue here? Simply this: taken at face value, Jesus' warning against calling any man father would not only seem to rule out calling a clergyman father, it would also keep us from using that title for earthly fathers and grandfathers, ancient Church Fathers, or even city fathers, would it not? For in reality, the Lord's statement, as it appears in the text, is that only one Person is ever to be called father, namely, our Father who is in heaven.

But was Christ's saying to be taken at face value? So few have ever done so. Or were we not to call Orthodox pastors father? If that is the case, several other passages in the Bible were immediately in trouble, including some statements by the Apostle Paul in the New Testament. To the Church at Corinth the Apostle wrote, "For if you were to have countless tutors in Christ, yet you would not have many fathers; for in Christ Jesus I became your *father* through the gospel" (I Corinthians 4:15, NASB, emphasis added). Does not Paul claim to be the spiritual father of the Corinthians—"Father Paul," if you please? Furthermore, he boldly refers to his spiritual ancestry as "our fathers" (I Corinthians 10:1).

And he did address earthly fathers in Colossae in this way: "Fathers, do not provoke your children, lest they become discouraged" (Colossians 3:21). It would appear the Apostle Paul certainly did not interpret the Lord Jesus Christ to say only One was to be called father, that is, the heavenly Father.

In addition to this, when the rich man saw Abraham in heaven with Lazarus in his bosom and addressed him as "Father Abraham," Abraham's response was not, "Do you not realize that only God the Father is to be called Father?" Rather, he replied, "Son, remember" (Luke 16:20-31).

Other Titles

But let us not stop here. For in addition to saying "only One is your Father," Jesus also declared, "Do not be called 'Rabbi' [or Teacher]; for One is your Teacher, the Christ" (Matthew 23:8). Yet Jesus Christ Himself acknowledged Nicodemus to be the "teacher of Israel" (John 3:10). And in the Church at Antioch certain men were called "prophets and teachers" (Acts 13:1).

Because the Apostle Paul recognized teachers as gifts of God to the Church, he also did not hesitate to call himself "a teacher of the Gentiles" (I Timothy 2:7). In this present day, almost all of us have at one time or another called certain people Sunday school teachers. At Dallas Seminary, one of the highest introductions a chapel speaker could receive was that of "a gifted Bible teacher." Thus the discussion goes far beyond any Protestant-Catholic lines.

Therefore, in saying we should call no one father and teacher, except God the Father and Christ Himself, the Lord Jesus appears not to be taking issue with the use of these particular titles in and of themselves.

It is the context of the passage itself which gives us the interpretive key we are looking for. In saying "call no man father," our Lord is contending with certain rabbis of His day who were using these specific titles to accomplish their own ends. And had these same apostate rabbis been using other titles like *reverend* and *pastor*, Jesus, it seems to me, would have said of these as well, "Call no one reverend or pastor."

What Did the Rabbis Mean?

To what ends, therefore, were the rabbis using the titles *father* and *teacher*? The answer revolves around at least two critical areas of leadership: teaching and personal character.

Consider first the teaching of these particular rabbis. They had begun their teaching at the right place, the Law of Moses. Said Jesus, "The scribes and the Pharisees sit in Moses' seat" (Matthew 23:2). Moses' Law was the true tradition—God had given it to Israel through Moses. The rabbis' responsibility was to preserve that tradition and faithfully pass it on to the next generation.

All too often, however, a rabbi would add his own grain of wisdom to the true tradition, thereby clouding it. Instead of passing down the sacred deposit along with the true interpretations of that deposit, he would add his own private interpretation. In turn his disciples, like their teacher, would do the same thing. Talk about the tradition of men, here it is all over again. (Some things never change, do they!)

The final outcome of all this was a human tradition that made the true Mosaic tradition of no effect. To these very rabbis Jesus had said, "For laying aside the commandment of God, you hold the tradition of men" (Mark 7:8). And again, "All too well you reject the commandment of God, that you may keep your tradition . . . making the word of God of no effect through your tradition which you have handed down" (Mark 7:9, 13).

In order to cut through all this innovative tradition which had gradually replaced the Mosaic tradition, and in order to bring people back to the truth, Jesus told His disciples, "But you, do not be called 'Rabbi.' " In other words, He was telling them not to use their positions as fathers and teachers as an opportunity to build disciples around their own private opinions. For to do so would only serve to "shut up the kingdom of heaven against men" (Matthew 23:13).

Instead, with the coming of Christ, these new rabbis— indeed all who would teach God's Word—were to faithfully hand down the true tradition of only one Rabbi: Christ Himself. The Bible calls this particular tradition, through the pen of the Apostle John, "the doctrine of Christ." In fact, as we noted earlier, this is why the specific teaching of the Twelve became known as "the Apostles' doctrine."

Since their time, successive generations of fathers and teachers in the Church have handed down and guarded the apostolic doctrine concerning Christ very carefully, for it represents the true interpretation of Holy Scripture.

This faithfulness to true Christian doctrine, by the way, can especially be seen in the Seven Ecumenical Councils of the Church, held between the fourth and eighth centuries.

It behooves anyone who claims to be a teacher of Christ's doctrine to be faithful to the Apostles' doctrine handed down through those Councils. Otherwise he runs the risk of inserting his own "private interpretation."

While it is true that all teachers of Christ's doctrine must begin at the right place, namely, the Holy Scriptures, it is also true that they should give the correct and true interpretation of Holy Scripture as passed down by holy and godly teachers and Fathers of the Church, especially in the Seven Councils.

Why are the Seven Ecumenical Councils so important? Because they point out what the Church universally held to be the true teaching concerning the Person of the Lord Jesus Christ and the Holy Trinity. They are faithful to what the Holy Scriptures teach concerning the one true Rabbi and Teacher, Jesus Christ. Teachers and fathers who teach private interpretations contrary to the doctrine of Christ as safeguarded in the Seven Ecumenical Councils should, I believe, not be recognized as true teachers and fathers.

The Rabbis and Personal Character

A second critical area of rabbinic leadership with which Jesus was concerned was personal character. He had detected a major flaw in the character of the scribes and Pharisees, a sin that might be called self-exaltation. They were using their position as fathers and teachers among God's people to exalt themselves. They wanted to be sure they received appropriate recognition—a carpeted office with adjoining half-bath, engraved personal stationery, and a silver four-door Buick! In light of this lack of character, Jesus said, "But he who is greatest among you shall be your servant. And whoever exalts himself will be humbled, and he who humbles himself will be exalted" (Matthew 23:11, 12).

Their self-exalting spirit had manifested itself in several ways. First, in hypocrisy. "For they say," said Jesus, "and do not do" (Matthew 23:3). All talk and no walk. Their talk was cheap because it was totally contradicted by their behavior. In pretense they would make long prayers, but in behavior devour widows' houses.

Second, they would make oaths, swearing by the gold of the temple rather than by the temple that sanctified the gold, thereby revealing their secret love of money. Although they paid tithes of mint, anise, and cumin, which they should have done gladly, they neglected the weightier matters of the law: justice, mercy, and faith.

Because they were hypocrites in these and numerous other ways, the Lord summed up His critique by saying, "Even so you also outwardly appear righteous to men, but inside you are full of hypocrisy and lawlessness" (Matthew 23:28). Plainly, their "insides" did not match their "outsides" because they were filled up with a self-exalting and self-serving spirit.

A third manifestation of their self-exalting spirit was the noticeable lack of godly service to others. "For," said Jesus, "they bind heavy burdens, hard to bear, and lay them on men's shoulders; but they themselves will not move them with one of their fingers" (Matthew 23:4).

No dirt was to be found under their fingernails, no mud on their uniforms. They were simply a group of lazy leaders who wanted to be served rather than to serve. No wonder, then, Jesus said not to be like them, for from God's standpoint, "he who is greatest among you shall be your servant" (Matthew 23:11).

A final manifestation of their self-exalting spirit was self-love, demonstrated by a desire to be seen by men. It was also shown by their love for the center seat at the head table at the feasts and in the synagogues and by their love of greetings in the marketplaces as people would call out, "Rabbi, Rabbi."

This self-love was a clear transgression of the Mosaic Law, which they professed to be keeping. For Moses' entire law could be summed up in the two great commandments, the greatest of which is, "You shall love the LORD your God with all your heart, with all your soul, and with all your mind" (Matthew 22:37). The second greatest is, "You shall love your neighbor as yourself" (Matthew 22:39).

Thus, these fathers and teachers were not leading their people into the love of God and neighbor. Quite to the contrary, they were exhibiting a self-exalting, self-serving spirit, filled up with a love for self.

The Verdict of Christ

It is in the face of the stench and shame of the apostasy of these religious leaders, therefore, that Jesus commanded the people, "Do not call anyone on earth your father; for One is your Father, He who is in heaven." While Father Abraham by his faithfulness deserved the title, as did others of Israel's greats in history, these rabbis had forfeited their role as fathers. They were to cease and desist in their use of the term and in turn bow to God Himself as the fountainhead of all fatherhood.

And in issuing His warning, Jesus addresses us today with the greatest of all commandments. He points us to the true fathers and teachers in His Church and to those who exhibit a love for God and love for their neighbors.

And What Are We to Do?

From the beginning of Church history, as was true

Photo by Fr. Marc Dunaway.

Seven former Campus Crusade for Christ leaders of the sixties meet in 1974 to form the New Covenant Apostolic Order, the core group that pursued Orthodox Christianity. Left to right: Richard Ballew, Gordon Walker, Jon Braun, Ray Nethery, Jack Sparks, Ken Berven, and Peter Gillquist.

Fr. Alexander Schmemann, right, visits with Fr. Weldon Hardenbrook in Santa Barbara, California, in the early 1980s.

Photo by Conciliar Press.

In February, 1979, the Evangelical Orthodox Church was founded as a denomination, and a synod of bishops established. Former EOC Bishops Jon Braun and Harold Dunaway exchange a joyful embrace as Peter Gillquist looks on.

Photo by Conciliar Press.

Photo by Fr. Marc Dunaway.

Fr. Richard Ballew conducts a baptismal service for the St. Athanasius parish of the Evangelical Orthodox Church, Santa Barbara, in the early 1980s.

Bishop MAXIMOS, left, and Fr. Peter Gillquist go over plans for the trip to Constantinople.

Photo by Conciliar Press.

Photo by Fr. Marc Dunaway.

Frs. Peter Gillquist, Gregory Wingenbach, and Richard Ballew at the head–quarters of the Patriarch of Constantinople in 1985.

Photo by Antiochian Orthodox Christian Archdiocese.

Metropolitan PHILIP Saliba
Primate
The Antiochian Orthodox Christian Archdiocese of North America.

Photo by Fr. George Corey.

His Beatitude IGNATIUS IV
Patriarch
of Antioch and all the East.

Patriarch IGNATIUS IV presides over a hierarchical liturgy at the patriarchal headquarters.

Photo by Antiochian Orthodox Christian Archdiocese.

Photo by Conciliar Press.

Orthodox scholar and author, Bishop KALLISTOS (Timothy Ware) visits with Fr. Peter Gillquist at the West Coast Clergy-Laity Conference of the Greek Orthodox Church in 1987.

Chrismations and Ordinations

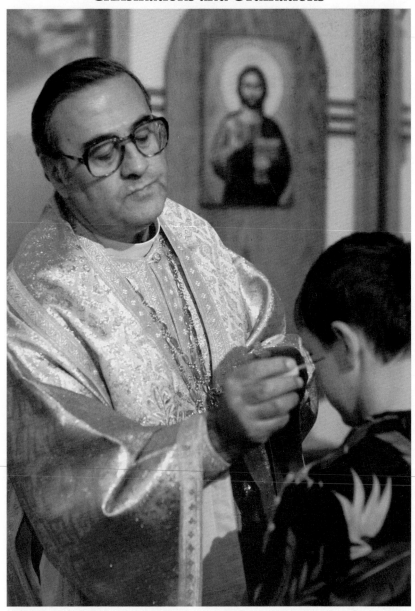

Photo by Conciliar Press.

Chrismations and ordinations began February 8, 1987 at Saint Michaels Church, Van Nuys, and continued the next Sunday at St. Nicholas Cathedral, Los Angeles. Here, Metropolitan PHILIP chrismates one of the young faithful.

Photo by Dawn Clodfelter.

"I wish I could go beyond words to describe to you the joy which I experienced as I was chrismating the little children of the Evangelical Orthodox faithful," Saidna PHILIP told the delegates at the Antiochian Archdiocesan Convention in July, 1987.

On to St. Peter & St. Paul Parish, Ben Lomond

Photo by Conciliar Press.

Metropolitan PHILIP begins the Divine Liturgy at St. Peter and St. Paul Church in Ben Lomond, California.

Photo by Conciliar Press.

Fr. Jack Sparks chrismates a child.

Photo by Conciliar Press.

Fr. Weldon Hardenbrook holds the Cross for veneration.

At St. John's Cathedral, Eagle River, Alaska

Photo by Robbie Clodfelter.

The faithful of St. John's designed and built the Church with their own labor.

Photo by Dianne Cranor.

Left to right: Archdeacon Hans, Fr. Jack Sparks, Metropolitan PHILIP, and Fr. Harold Dunaway in front of the Cathedral of St. John the Evangelist.

Photo by Myles Kelly.

The procession of the cross outside St. John's Orthodox Cathedral.

St. Ignatius Parish, Nashville, Tennessee

Photo by Callie Shell.

Fr. Gordon Walker is ordained at St. Ignatius Church, Nashville, Tennessee. "Do Thou, Lord of all men, preserve in pureness of life and unswerving faith this man upon whom, through me, you have graciously been pleased to lay hands."

The Next Six Years

Photo by Bill Dunniway.

Recent convert to Orthodoxy, Frank Schaeffer, speaks to St. Peter & St. Paul Orthodox Church in Ben Lomond, California, in 1990.

Photo by Conciliar Press.

His Grace, Bishop BASIL chrismating new members of St. Athanasius Orthodox Church in Goleta, California.

Photo by Conciliar Press.

A planning meeting for the Department of Missions and Evangelism. From left: Frs. Gordon Walker, Peter Gillquist, Michael Keiser, and Jon Braun.

Photo by Dimitrios Panagos.

Hierarchs gather during visit of Patriarch ALEKSY II (Patriarch of Moscow and All Russia) to America, fall, 1991. Left to right: Bishop ANTOUN, Metropolitan THEODOSIUS, Patriarch ALEKSY, Metropolitan PHILIP.

Photo by Fr. David Ogan.

Fr. Peter Gillquist preaching the Gospel in a Romanian Cathedral during a 1992 evangelism tour.

Photo by Conciliar Press.

1992 Pan-Orthodox Conference on Missions and Evangelism in Santa Barbara, California, held each year over the Labor Day weekend.

"Brothers and Sisters in Christ, Welcome Home!"

Photo by Dianne Cranor.

throughout Israel, those anointed by God for service were called by certain names: *prophet, teacher, rabbi* (in Israel), and *father*. In that same spirit, other titles have emerged, like *reverend, pastor, professor,* or *brother* (for some evangelical pastors and Catholic monks). These designations speak both of warmth and dignity.

Just as in our family units there is one who with love is called father, so in God's household we have and will continue to honor those who have brought us to the new birth through our Lord Jesus Christ. Indeed, what better term for them than *father?*

Jesus warned against calling unworthy men father or teacher in order that the leadership of His holy nation would remain pure. Whether they be bishop, father, teacher, deacon, or pastor, all must remain faithful to the true doctrine of Christ and manifest a personal character befitting godly humility that leads the Church into the love of God the Holy Trinity and of one's neighbor.

As a priest myself, I find a personal zone of comfort in calling an older fellow-priest father, for I really view him as such. In the parish itself the title is a warm and intimate line of demarcation that distinguishes (not separates) those in the body of Christ called to lead and give care.

In our journey, when we agreed to use the term *father* as a proper designation for the priest, we told the people they were certainly free to continue to use the term *pastor* if they were more at ease doing so. Soon, the more natural term came to be *father*, and that is what is used today.

Two things have resulted. The people know there is a spiritual "head of the house" who is there to image the headship of Jesus Christ and pass on His mercy and love. In addition, being called father keeps the clergy reminded of who they are: not just good speakers or administrators or rulers or exhorters—but primarily fathers, daddies, papas to the people of God. If they are that, then the rest of what they are is in far better perspective.

8

FACING UP TO MARY

I t is safe to say that no woman in history is more mis–understood by modern Christendom than the Virgin Mary.

And it is also probable that in a disagreement concerning Mary between two Christians, if their differences remain unresolved, it will be due in large part to stubborn refusal to deal with the biblical data.

If I have heard him say it once, I have heard Billy Graham say it at least a half dozen times over the years: "We evangelical Christians do not give Mary her proper due."

His statement raises the crucial question about Mary. What is her proper due? Before we look to the Scriptures for some answers, let us acknowledge right up front a problem which makes our task much more difficult than it should be.

The highly charged emotional atmosphere which surrounds this subject serves to blunt our objectivity in facing up to Mary. Many of us were brought up to question or reject honor paid to Mary in Christian worship and art. Therefore, we often have our minds made up in advance.

We have allowed our preconceptions to color our under-standing even of the Scripture passages concerning her. We have not let the facts speak for themselves.

As my associates and I attempted to face up to Mary honestly and openly—and it was not easy for us—we turned first to the Bible and specifically to the New Testament. Then we went to the Old Testament. As we studied we also considered what the early Church Fathers had to say on the subject. We looked at the whole of Church history to try to understand both how she had been prop-erly honored, and how incorrect dogmas concerning her crept into the picture.

The New Testament Record

What is it, then, that the New Testament teaches con-cerning the Virgin Mary? We can find at least four crucial answers.

Mary Is the Greatest Woman Who Ever Lived

Whereas our Lord Jesus Christ told us there was no greater man to walk the earth than John the Baptist, both the Archangel Gabriel and the saintly Elizabeth confessed to Mary, "Blessed are you among women" (Luke 1:28, 42).

She is the most blessed of women for several reasons, the greatest of which is that she conceived, carried, gave birth to, and nurtured the very Savior of our souls. The One who today occupies the heavenly throne of David and is seated regally at the right hand of God the Father, entered the human race and became our Savior through her womb. She was chosen by the Father to bear His only-begotten Son.

In that role, Mary was the first person in all history to receive and accept Christ as her Savior. You and I are called to enthrone the Lord in our hearts and lives—to follow Mary's example in doing so. Early in Christian history she is called "the first of the redeemed."

I remember entering a Church in suburban Chicago some years ago and seeing a painting or icon of Mary with open arms front and center on the wall (the apse) just behind the altar. My first impulse was to wonder why Christ alone was not featured at that particular place in the Church, though He was shown in a large circle that was super-imposed over her heart.

When I asked why she was so prominently featured, the Christian scholar with me explained: "This is one of the greatest evangelistic icons in the entire Church. What you see is Christ living as Lord in Mary's life, and her outstretched arms are an invitation to you and me to let Him live in our lives as He has in hers." The power of that icon stays in my mind to this day. For she has set the example for all of us to personally give our lives over fully to Jesus Christ.

Mary is also blessed because she found favor in the sight of God. Gabriel's words of encouragement to her were, "Rejoice, highly favored one, the Lord is with you" (Luke 1:28). Then he comforted her by saying, "Do not be afraid, Mary, *for you have found favor with God*" (Luke 1:30, emphasis added).

What does one do to become one of God's favorites, to be rewarded by Him? Remember Cornelius in Acts 10? He was the first Gentile to convert to Christ, "a devout man and one . . . who gave alms generously to the people, and prayed to God always" (Acts 10:2). Two verses later he was told in a vision, "Your prayers and your alms have come up for a memorial before God." The Lord took notice of his deeds of devotion and brought him salvation. In a similar way, Mary's purity found favor with

God, and she was chosen to bear His Son.

Am I suggesting human merit earns salvation? Not at all. As commendable as it is for us to live in purity, a devout life never merits salvation. Otherwise why would Mary be called first of the *redeemed*, or why would Cornelius need to be *baptized* into Christ by Saint Peter? Prayer and devotion, however, do gain God's attention. When we seek Him with all our hearts, we do find Him! When we give Him everything we have, our very life, we will be favored of God. This is precisely what Mary did, and why she is to be considered the greatest woman who ever lived.

Mary Is Our Model for the Christian Life

The Orthodox Church has taught from the very beginning that Mary is the supreme example, or prototype, of what happens to a person who fully places trust and faith in God. Everything we aspire to become in Christ, she already is. We are all to "receive" Christ (John 1:12). And as we noted previously, Mary was the first human being who did receive Christ. Out of the millions of "decisions" made for Christ, Mary's was the first. Therefore, whatever promises the Holy Scriptures hold for us, Mary already possesses.

Our model of obedience. While God certainly knew Mary desired to please Him, He did not take her servitude for granted. The angel explained how she would bear Christ. "The Holy Spirit will come upon you, and the power of the Highest [God the Father] will overshadow you; therefore, also, that Holy One who is to be born will be called the Son of God" (Luke 1:35).

Now Mary had a decision to make. Was she willing? Hear her answer, for it is the doorway to the life of spiritual service for all of us. "Behold the maidservant of the Lord!" she said. "Let it be to me according to your word" (Luke 1:38). Even if we are totally sincere about wanting to follow God, He will never conscript us apart from our consent! Like Mary, we are to choose freely to obey Him and do His will.

Some thirty years later, by the way, Mary again had opportunity to exalt her Lord. She was with Jesus at a wedding in Cana of Galilee. The servants who were in charge of the celebration discovered they were out of wine. Mary had no doubt as to who could solve their problem. Referring to her Son, the Lord Jesus Christ, she advised them, "Whatever He says to you, do it" (John 2:5). In all her life Mary practiced this advice she gave to the servants. That is why she stands as our example of Christian obedience.

Our model of purity and holiness. We who are called holy brethren (Hebrews 3:1) are commanded to be holy as God is holy (I Peter 1:15, 16). We are to present our bodies as a living sacrifice (Romans 12:1). Is it so unthinkable that she whose holy body was the recipient of God Incarnate should be called "most holy" by the Church?

If we as the Church are called to be without "spot or wrinkle or any such thing, but that she should be holy and without blemish" (Ephesians 5:27), does it not follow that she who is the birth-giver of the Lord of that Church should be of that same holy character? Certainly we should be able to look to Mary as our example of holiness and purity.

Our model of royalty and intercession. If the sacred Scriptures declare that we are all kings (Revelation 1:6), is it so strange that the Church refers to Mary as Queen? If the Holy Bible promises that you and I shall judge angels (I

Corinthians 6:3), is it so odd that the Church should sing that Mary is "more honorable than the cherubim and more glorious beyond compare than the seraphim"?

Not only has Mary by the mercy and power of God conquered both sin and death, the psalmist sees a glimpse of her in heaven through prophetic eyes. For in Psalm 45:9, Christ is King and Mary is at His side as Queen—and rightly so. If God can make us "kings and priests" (Revelation 1:6) for all eternity, certainly He has the prerogative to crown her with higher honor in heaven's royal procession.

If Saint Paul instructs us as a holy priesthood to pray "always . . . for all the saints" (Ephesians 6:18), is it so outrageous to confess with the Church that holy Mary (along with all the saints who have passed from death to life and continually stand in the presence of Christ) intercedes before her Son on behalf of all men? For Mary is the prototype of what we are all called to be.

Mary Is the Mother of God

Now things get a bit more touchy for some of us. Here is one of those emotional trouble spots I mentioned earlier. Whether we like to face it or not, the Bible teaches Mary is the Mother of God. Let's first look at the text, then we will discuss why this title is so important to our lives as Christians in the Church.

After Christ had been conceived in her womb, Mary paid a visit to the home of relatives Zacharias and Elizabeth, parents of soon-to-be-born John the Baptist. When Mary greeted her cousin, Elizabeth called her blessed and said, "Why is this granted to me, that the *mother of my Lord* should come to me?" (Luke 1:43, emphasis added). Elizabeth knew that her Lord, the Messiah of Israel, was God. She knew from childhood, "Hear, O Israel:

The LORD our God, the LORD is one!" (Deuteronomy 6:4). And she knew that her Lord was in the womb of Mary.

This title, Mother of God, took on great importance in the fourth century, when a heretic named Nestorius—a man who held high office in the Church—claimed the one in Mary's womb was certainly man, but that He was not God. Orthodox Christians, with one accord, said, "Wrong!" To see Jesus Christ as something less than God in the flesh is sub-Christian. For unless the one in Mary's womb was and is God, we are dead in our sins. To safeguard the full deity of Christ, the Church has always insisted that Mary be rightly called—as Elizabeth discerned her to be—the Mother of God.

This title, of course, does not mean mother of the Holy Trinity, for the Holy Trinity has no mother. Neither does it mean she originated the Person who is God the Son for He exists before all time. It refers instead to Mary being the God-bearer (*Theotokos* in Greek), Mother of the eternal Son of God, who assumed full humanity in her womb.

When a man buys a large plot of land and turns cattle out to graze on it, he fences in his acreage. He does so to protect his cattle, to keep them from wandering off, and to discourage rustlers. Similarly, the Church sets doctrinal fences around its foundational truths. And nothing is more basic and important to us than the deity of Christ. Because Christ is God, we set a firm and non-negotiable fence around His divinity by our unmovable confession that Mary is the Mother of God.

Just as we insist on the Virgin Birth of Christ, we also insist that for the nine months she carried Him in His humanity, He was at every moment fully God as well. Thus we say boldly and with great insistence that Mary is the Mother of God, Theotokos, God-bearer. To say

anything less is to side with those who deny Christ's
deity.

We Are to Honor Mary and Call Her Blessed

Now comes the toughest test of all. Not only is Mary the
most blessed of women, our model for the Christian life,
and the Mother of God, but we are also called to honor her
and to bless her. How do we know? The Bible tells us so.

During her three-month stay at Elizabeth's house,
Mary offered one of the most beautiful prayers of praise to
the Lord in all the Scriptures. It begins, "My soul magnifies
the Lord"; thus it has become known as "The Magnificat."

In that prayer, inspired by the Holy Spirit, Mary prophesied, "henceforth all generations will call me blessed"
(Luke 1:48). Essentially, all generations in Church history
have done so; only those of the last few centuries have
faltered. Our generation of American Christians is filled
with those who refuse to bless her, and we must change our
ways.

From the beginning of recorded Christian worship,
Orthodox Christians have taken special care to venerate or
honor Mary in the Liturgy. There is an ancient hymn which
begins, "It is truly right to bless you, O Theotokos [Mother
of God]." She is also called in this hymn "ever-blessed and
most pure." The biblical injunction to honor Mary is followed and taken seriously.

We do not, of course, worship Mary, for worship is
reserved for the Trinity: Father, Son, and Holy Spirit. But
she is most certainly to be honored and venerated. And
because Christ is our elder brother, the firstborn of many
brethren, we honor the Virgin Mary as our Mother, our
Lady, as well. Just as Eve was mother of the old Adamic
race, so Mary is the true Mother of the new race, the Body
of Christ, the Church.

Perhaps in part because we refuse to honor Mary, our generation seems to struggle with honoring *anyone*. For example, next time a presidential news conference comes on T.V., watch closely how some in the press corps behave! Far from merely trying to get the story, many are out for intimidation and willful dishonor.

While God's Word tells us to honor the king (I Peter 2:17) and to give preference to each other (Romans 12:10), our generation seems to delight in challenging and humiliating other people, especially those in authority. Not only are we who are Bible-believing Christians urged to give honor to whom honor is due (see Romans 13:7), we are called by God in no uncertain terms to bless the Mother of our God. We cannot get around that point in Scripture.

The Old Testament and the Virgin

We know that the Old Testament is more than just an inspired account of the history of mankind, or of Israel in particular. In its pages—indeed central to its message—is also the prophetic record concerning the coming of our Lord Jesus Christ. He is typified throughout. Adam was a type of Christ as head of the human race. Moses was a type of Christ, in that he led the people out of bondage into the land of promise. David typified Christ as King of Israel.

Often overlooked, however, is the fact that the Virgin Mary is also seen in the prophetic pages of the Old Testament. Most Christians are aware that the Prophet Isaiah predicts Mary's virgin conception of Christ when he writes: "Therefore the Lord Himself will give you a sign: Behold, the virgin shall conceive and bear a Son, and shall call His name Immanuel" (Isaiah 7:14). But there are numerous other passages which speak of Mary as well.

Ever-Virgin

From the very early years of the Church, Mary was called not only Virgin, but *Ever-Virgin*. She was seen as never having had a sexual union with Joseph, before or after the birth of Christ. Ezekiel 44:1, 2 is a passage often referred to by the early Fathers in this regard. It states: "Then He brought me back to the outer gate of the sanctuary which faces toward the east, but it was shut. And the LORD said to me, 'This gate shall be shut; it shall not be opened, and no man shall enter by it, because the LORD God of Israel has entered by it; therefore it shall be shut.'"

In traditional interpretation of this passage, Mary is the temple and Christ is the Prince of Peace. The gate mentioned is seen as a picture of the door of Mary's womb through which Christ entered our world. You might not find that interpretation in some of today's commentaries, but it was held by the great majority of early Church Fathers, as well as many of the Reformation leaders—notably Martin Luther.

Virgin Until

At this point, however, a very valid question can be raised. If she remained a virgin, why does the Gospel of Matthew tell us that Joseph knew not his wife *until* after Christ was born (see Matthew 1:25)?

From a Scriptural standpoint, the presence of the phrase "till she had brought forth her firstborn Son," does not automatically mean that Joseph must have had a sexual union with her afterward. In both Greek and Hebrew the word *until* (or *till* or *to*) can have several meanings. We find it in II Samuel 6:23: "Michal the daughter of Saul had no children *to* (until) the day of her death." It is used again in Matthew 28:20 where the risen Christ says, "Lo, I am with you always, even *to* (until) the end of the age." And in

Deuteronomy 34:6 we read, "[Moses was buried] in a valley in the land of Moab... but no one knows his grave *to* (until) this day."

Obviously the use of the word in these passages does not imply that Michal had a child after her death, that Christ will no longer be with us at the end of the world, or that Moses' burial place was discovered the day Deuteronomy 34:6 was written. By the same token, the word *until* in Matthew 1:25 does not mean that Joseph and Mary began a sexual union after Christ was born. Such a teaching is found nowhere in Scripture and is contrary to the consistent voice of the entire early Church.

Christ's Brothers and Sisters

But doesn't the Bible also mention the brothers and sisters of Christ? Who were they and where did they come from?

For one thing, the Scriptures never call them the sons and daughters of Mary and Joseph. In several passages the Bible speaks of near relatives as "brothers." Abraham and Lot were called brothers, although Lot was actually Abraham's nephew. And Jacob and Laban were called brothers, even though Jacob was the son of Rebecca, Laban's sister.

Scripture is therefore silent concerning the nature of this relationship between Christ and these brothers and sisters. Early Fathers differed slightly in their understanding of what the terms meant. Some, such as Saint Ambrose, believed that the "brothers" were children of a former marriage between Joseph and a wife who died prior to the events of Matthew, chapter 1. Others taught that the "brothers" were cousins. But on one point, almost everyone is in agreement: Mary and Joseph had no sexual union whatsoever, before or after the birth of Christ.

I must say in all candor that had my betrothed been the woman chosen by the Father to bear His eternal Son in the flesh, my view of her would have been utterly transformed, and my honor for her infinitely heightened. Imagine being engaged to the Mother of God! It was so with Joseph. His betrothed was ever-virgin.

Other Traditions—True and False

There are two other beliefs concerning Mary that must be briefly mentioned and addressed. The first is her bodily assumption into heaven, the other her immaculate conception.

The Assumption of the Virgin

It was widely reported in the early Church that shortly after her death, Mary's body was assumed into heaven. In later centuries, the Roman Church ratified this belief as dogma, while the Eastern Church withheld such an official imprimatur. Most Christians agree that such a miracle is within the realm of firm biblical precedent, Enoch and Elijah being two examples. Further, there is no known record of any relics of the Holy Virgin. The assumption of the Virgin can be safely seen and honored as an historic Christian tradition, though not recorded in the Scriptures.

The Immaculate Conception of Mary

However, the Immaculate Conception of Mary is a doctrine unknown in the ancient Church and unique to the modern Roman Church. In an effort to distance Mary (and protect Christ) from the stain of sin, the Immaculate Conception holds that Mary was conceived and born without original sin. This teaching has no basis either in Scripture or in the Creeds of the Church.

Whatever other excesses may have cropped up in history, even the Roman Church has never officially believed or taught that Mary was in any way coequal with the Trinity or was to be worshiped with the Trinity. Such allegations are sometimes set forth by critics of the Roman Church, but without basis in fact.

Mary and Salvation

Near the end of the Vespers service in the Orthodox Church, the officiant says, "O holy Mother of God, save us." Can Mary really save us? Yes, and here is why.

Certainly, we believe that Mary is pure and holy, that she rules with Christ, that she even prays for us. We know that Mary relinquished her will to the will of God, thus cooperating fully with the purpose of God. And we know that it is the express purpose of God to save those who have faith in Christ. At the very least we can say that Mary is concerned about our salvation and that she desires it. That should be true of all believers.

So the original question, "Can Mary save *us?*" leads to another question: "Can we save others?" Again, the Holy Scriptures speak with resounding clarity. Here are some examples:

> Take heed to yourself and to the doctrine. Continue in them, for in doing this you will save both yourself and those who hear you (I Timothy 4:16).

> Let him know that he who turns a sinner from the error of his way will save a soul from death and cover a multitude of sins (James 5:20).

> And on some have compassion, making a distinction; but

others save with fear, pulling them out of the fire (Jude 22, 23).

Fire saves (I Corinthians 3:15); prayer saves (James 5:15); angels save (Isaiah 63:9); baptism saves (I Peter 3:21); preaching saves (I Corinthians 1:21); the Apostle Paul saves (Romans 11:14).

New life in Christ, or salvation, is both personal union with Him and an incorporation into the wholeness of the Body, the Church. Salvation is a Church affair, a Church concern, because we are all affected by it. Therefore, in Christ we all have a part to play in the corporate nature of His saving act.

We do not save alone; Mary does not save alone. Jesus Christ is our wellspring of salvation. He said, "Without Me you can do nothing" (John 15:5). And "If you abide in Me, and My words abide in you, you will ask what you desire, and it shall be done for you" (John 15:7).

Mary has a participatory role in our salvation because she provided the body of Christ and thereby became the "mother" of all those who would be saved. That is why Jesus, while on the Cross, said to His mother, "Woman, behold your son!" and then said to Saint John, "Behold your mother!" (John 19:26, 27). Understood in this way, does the Mother of God save us? Thank God, *yes!*

Changing Our Mind About Mary

Many Christians have been grossly misinformed in the last 150 years concerning the historical Church's view of Mary. We have forgotten she is favored by the Father, and is the model—indeed, the flagship—of all humanity. She was the only one who gave her flesh to the Son of God, and she is uniquely to be blessed throughout all generations (Luke 1:48).

What we do about Mary is connected directly to what we do about the Church. The community of Christ's followers is called to act together. Taking action with regard to Mary is not simply personal or private; it has to do with responding as the Church.

And where in Christendom has the fullness of truth concerning Mary been preserved? Even most Protestants—both liberal and conservative—know she is slighted in their circles. The answer for Protestants who take the biblical and historical evidence seriously lies neither within the Protestant Churches nor in the Roman Church with its questionable late dogmatic additions concerning Mary.

The answer lies in the historic Orthodox Church, which has maintained the biblical fidelity concerning Mary. The hour is at hand for all of us who love Christ and take seriously the Holy Scriptures to set our hearts and minds to giving Holy Mary her proper due in the proper Church. We do so because God has done great things for and through her (Luke 1:49).

As Christians we do not live by feelings, we live by faith. Let us once for all rise above those fears the devil has sown in our hearts to neutralize us against this precious woman who gave birth to our Savior. Bless her in the midst of God's people. Follow her example in exalting Christ. Confess her as the Mother of God. Come home to the Church that has kept intact our holy faith. And may we help turn our generation back to the honoring and blessing of Mary which God has commanded.

9

A SIGN FOR ALL CHRISTIANS

Years ago on an Easter Sunday—I must have been seven or eight years of age—we went out for dinner after Church to a hotel restaurant. About the time we placed our order, I recall looking up and seeing the family at a table across from us bow in prayer before eating and make the sign of the cross. My response was bewilderment. *What does that mean?* I thought to myself.

Not many years later, at the Minneapolis Auditorium, I attended one of my first Lakers' games. (Yes, the L.A. Lakers used to be the Minneapolis Lakers. Who has ever heard of lakes in L.A.?) At one point in the game, center George Mikan stepped up to the free-throw line for a foul shot and crossed himself before attempting the free throw. *What is this?* I thought as he went two for two. *Is this some sort of rabbit's foot gesture?* What is this sign of the cross anyway?

Or let's ask the question another way. What is the most well-known symbol of all time? Anyone we ask—philosopher, historian, or artist—each would most likely respond, "the cross." This familiar symbol is found in all aspects of the life of each person, from birth to grave.

History was dramatically changed not only by the impact of the Crucifixion itself, but by a visual manifestation of the cross to the Roman Emperor, Constantine. Granted a vision of the sign of the cross in the heavens, he was converted, and in A.D. 312 he brought to an end a long, torturous period of persecution of Christians.

How could two simple lines that even a child could draw, one horizontal, the other vertical, cause kings to change the course of history, yet give Christian families such hope and comfort at the death of their loved ones as they bid farewell? Is it just a symbol? Or is something more powerful and effective to be found within the spiritual application of this symbol? I believe there is much more in the cross than many present-day Christians are led to understand. And I believe a biblical rediscovery of the cross is essential to the spiritual health of each Christian.

A Sign of Triumph

It is the Person of the Lord Jesus Christ that makes the cross so powerful, so meaningful, and so essential to our salvation. Our Lord, who took upon Himself our complete humanity, also, in that flesh, took upon Himself a common form of Roman execution and made the cross once and for all the glory and victory for all believers.

The Scriptures say that Christ, in His death, "wiped out the handwriting of requirements that was against us, which was contrary to us. And He has taken it out of the way, having nailed it to the cross" (Colossians 2:14).

Imagine what incredible power stands between us and death, between us and the clutches of the kingdom of darkness, between us and everlasting hell. Yes, the cross is more than a symbol for earthly decor; it is the weapon of peace that sets us free from being slaves to sin, death, and the devil.

No wonder the Apostle Paul shouted out in faith, "But God forbid that I should boast except in the cross of our Lord Jesus Christ, by whom the world has been crucified to me, and I to the world" (Galatians 6:14). The reality of the cross was sealed on the breast of Paul, who was able to stand against the schemes of the evil one and run the race to the finish. "For the message of the cross is foolishness to those who are perishing, but to us who are being saved it is the power of God" (I Corinthians 1:18).

A Sign for All Centuries

Let's go back to the centuries when the Church was not divided and see if those early Christians felt as strongly as the Apostle Paul about the cross.

In Christianity's second century we find Tertullian (A.D. 145–220) saying, "In all travels and movements, in all our coming in and going out, in putting on our shoes, at the bath, at the table, in lighting our candles, in lying down, in sitting down, whatever employment occupies us, we mark our forehead with the sign of the cross" (*On the Soldier's Crown*, chapter 3).

About a century later, the great Saint Athanasius recorded, "by the sign of the cross. . .all magic is stayed, all sorcery confounded, all the idols are abandoned and deserted, and all senseless pleasure ceases, as the eye of faith looks up to heaven from the earth" (*On the Incarnation*, IV, 31).

Saint Cyril of Jerusalem (A.D. 315–386) was even more insistent on the use of the sign of the cross:

Let us not be ashamed to confess the Crucified. Let the cross as our seal be boldly made with our fingers upon our brow, and on all occasions; over the bread we eat; over the cups we drink; in our comings and in our goings; before sleep; on lying down and rising up; when we are on the way and when we are still. It is a powerful safeguard; it is without price, for the sake of the poor; without toil, because of the sick; for it is a grace from God, a badge of the faithful, and a terror to devils; for He displayed them openly, leading them away in triumph by the force of it [Colossians 2:15]. For when they see the cross, they are reminded of the Crucified; they fear Him who had smashed the heads of dragons [Psalm 73:13]. Despise not the seal as a free gift, but rather for this reason honor your Lord all the more. *(Catechesis*, XIII, chapter 36)

Martin Luther, who is called the Father of the Protestant Reformation, called on his flock to use the sign of the cross. For example, in his instructions on morning prayers he wrote, "In the morning, when you rise, make the sign of the cross and say, 'In the name of God the Father, the Son, and the Holy Spirit. Amen' " (Martin Luther, *Small Catechism*, VII, 1).

A Sign Neglected

Astonishingly, it was not until the seventeenth century, at the time of King James, that a small group of Puritans began writing and speaking against the use of the sign of the cross. Reacting to the ills of the medieval Roman Church, they believed it to be a human invention which catered to superstition. These same English Puritans, who significantly influenced the North American continent, deserted one of the most powerful and cherished weapons of the entire history of the Church. *Romophobia* was their mentor.

Today, many American Christians have been deceived by the actions of a vocal minority and have become ashamed of the glory of the cross signed upon their breasts. But hungry for a way to physically express their allegiance to Christ, many of those who reject making the sign of the cross have ended up creating their own Christian hand signs.

I remember so well the "Jesus Movement" days when many of us were trying to come up with a common sign to use to set us apart from the student movement which powerfully used the peace sign. One day in 1970, a close friend got the idea of the "one way" sign, which was inspired by the doctrine of Jesus Christ being the only way to God. Thousands of posters were printed and distributed and soon this "one way sign" was employed by Christians all over the world. Even Billy Graham was portrayed in a national magazine demonstrating the sign in Greenwich Village.

The "one way" sign did help Christians to identify with each other. But it didn't last. I still see it used by a few diehards, but it will soon be gone. Why? It wasn't Orthodox; it wasn't the Church's sign. It wasn't the sign of the cross. The insignia of Jesus is not a raised index finger, but the cross: the true sign of every Christian.

Making signs on one's person is not a distinctly Christian activity. In 1892, the American government adopted a ceremony from a patriotic magazine called *Youth's Companion* and soon after required by law that every student in the public education system salute the American flag. Until just recently students were expelled from their classrooms if they refused to honor their country in this way. Even today, most Christians in America would suspect the loyalty of anyone who rejected the patriotic demonstration of placing the hand over the heart as the salute to the flag. Yet many of these same Christian people are bothered and ashamed to use the sign of the cross on their breasts. They refuse to use it, writing it off as some Roman or pagan holdover. How great the loss they suffer!

A Sign with Power

Although some may say signs have no real power, signs have always been significant to the people of God. Remember the occasion of the first Passover as recorded in the Old Testament? God instructed the Israelites to "take some of the blood and put it on the two doorposts and on the lintel of the houses where they eat it" (Exodus 12:7). He promised, "For I will pass through the land of Egypt on that night, and will strike all the firstborn in the land of Egypt, both man and beast; and against all the gods of Egypt I will execute judgment: I am the LORD. Now the blood shall be a sign for you on the houses where you are. And when I see the blood, I will pass over you; and the plague shall not be on you to destroy you when I strike the land of Egypt" (Exodus 12:12, 13).

What is remarkable in this is that the sign of the blood on the doorposts was no mere symbol. It was a symbol with power—so much so that it kept the death angel from destroying the firstborn children of Israel. Imagine, then, the power of the living cross which bore our Savior's death as we apply it to our hearts.

Recall the time in the wilderness when the children of Israel were perishing from the bite of poisonous snakes because of their rebellion. God told Moses, "Make a fiery serpent, and set it on a pole; and it shall be that everyone who is bitten, when he looks at it, shall live" (Numbers 21:8). As incredible as that sounds to modern man, the people who looked lived! That is what Jesus was teaching the Pharisee, Nicodemus, when He said, "And as Moses lifted up the serpent in the wilderness, even so must the Son of Man be lifted up" (John 3:14). Lifted up on what? The cross! If the Israelites were healed by looking at a fiery serpent lifted up on a pole, how much more healing will come to those who bear the Christian sign of the cross? That's why the Apostle Paul says he glories in the cross.

A Sign on Ourselves

By the cross of Christ, Satan was defeated, our sins were canceled out, the sacrifice was made in full. By identifying ourselves with the cross, we flash our new identification cards, as it were, before sin, death, and the evil one. And when temptation comes, or when our bodies want to take over the controls with their passions, physically making a cross on ourselves brings the power of the cross into action like an arrow released from a bow.

And how is the sign of the cross traditionally made by Orthodox Christians? We hold our thumb and first two fingers of our right hand together. This speaks of the three Persons in the Holy Trinity. Then, the last two fingers are held against the heel of our hand. These speak of the two natures of Jesus Christ: His full divinity and full humanity. In this, we hold the truth of the Gospel in our hand. And with it we touch in succession our forehead, middle chest, right shoulder, and finally our left shoulder. We thus apply the cross to our mind, our heart, and our strength.

On our journey to Orthodoxy, Jack Sparks wrote an article entitled "The Sign of the Cross." He summarized the centrality of the sign of the cross as follows:

1. It has been, and still is the practice of the overwhelming majority of your fellow Christians—many of whom died for the faith to help preserve the Gospel of Jesus Christ for you to believe. If we truly believe our Lord's words in John 17 that the Church is to be one, then why should we not utilize the sign of the cross as our forefathers have done?

2. We freely use the symbol of the cross atop our church buildings, on our lecterns, altars, bulletins, and imprinted on our Bibles. Why not use it on ourselves—the people for whom Christ died—as well?

3. Using the sign of the cross gives us a personal, physical, and visible means to glory in the cross. Apart from actually doing something specific, one is hard-pressed to glory in the cross of Christ mentally. We use our voices and lips to tell others of the cross. Why should we withhold our hands and arms, which God has also given us, from doing the same? This is all part of glorifying God in our bodies. (Jack Sparks, "The Sign of the Cross," *New Oxford Review*, January-February, 1982)

If we will but use the sign to express reverence for the Father, Son, and Holy Spirit—to remind ourselves of God's presence—this will go a long way toward helping us both to do good and to avoid sin. For the cross is our weapon of peace and our power to live holier lives. Satan and his demons fear the cross. Its sign, therefore, can be a means of protection for the children of God.

The fourth-century saint, John Chrysostom, said, "When therefore you sign yourself, think of the purpose of the cross, and quench any anger and all other passions. Consider the price that has been paid for you" (*Commentary on Matthew*, Homily 54).

PART THREE

THE GREAT ENTRANCE

10

A DECADE OF DECISION

Unlike almost everyone else who has discovered her, we found the Orthodox Church in history books. We had studied the New Testament, the early Fathers and councils, and the Great Schism. We made our choice. The East had kept the fullness of apostolic Christianity.

But we had not yet met the Orthodox Church as she existed in our time. What was she like? Would she be receptive to us? Most importantly, was she vital, committed, spiritually alive—in short, was she still Orthodox?

First Contacts

John Bartke grew up in a conservative Presbyterian congregation, and his family later transferred to the Evangelical Free Church. When he was a junior in high school in 1969, he wandered into a Bible study group led by Jack Sparks in Berkeley, California. For two years, before leaving for college, John was a frequent participant in the study group. He ended up on the mailing list of the Chris-

tian World Liberation Front (CWLF), the organization Jack
Sparks had founded as an outreach to the Berkeley
counter-culture.

Through a personal search for a deeper experience of
the Church, Bartke became an Orthodox Christian just
before his senior year in college. He went straight from
undergraduate school to Saint Vladimir's Seminary in
suburban New York City, a school operated by the Orthodox Church in America (OCA), the American outgrowth
of the Russian Orthodox Church. He remained on the
CWLF mailing list.

By 1976, the CWLF mail began to look more Orthodox.
There was talk of sacrament, councils, and creeds. Bartke
wrote his old Bible teacher for more information. Jack
Sparks sent some preliminary study papers in early 1977
with specific instruction not to pass them around: they
were unedited first drafts. John read them through and
immediately brought them to Fr. Alexander Schmemann,
dean of the seminary. "These things are Orthodox!" he
announced to Fr. Schmemann, after filling him in on his
friendship with Jack Sparks.

Fr. Schmemann placed a call to Bishop Dmitri, who as
a teenager had converted to Orthodoxy from a Southern
Baptist background back in Texas. He was then over-
seeing the Diocese of the West for the OCA. "Several of
these men are living near Santa Barbara. They're a group
of evangelical Christians who appear to be discovering
the Orthodox Church. Could I suggest you go see them?"
Fr. Schmemann asked.

Later that spring, Bishop Dmitri phoned Fr. Ted Wojcik,
pastor of Saint Innocent Orthodox Church in the Los
Angeles suburb of Tarzana, and asked him to pay a call to
Santa Barbara. With Lent, followed by graduations and
summer vacation, it was not until early fall that Fr. Ted

was able to make the trip.

When he arrived in Santa Barbara in the fall of 1977, Fr. Ted stopped at a phone booth, telephoned the Sparks' home and discovered that Jack was at the newly formed Academy of Orthodox Theology conducting classes. Fr. Richard Ballew recalls that he was in the middle of his lecture on the Arian controversy when "in walked this priest, unknown to any of us, who calmly sat down and listened to the lecture along with the students. After class, introductions were made and we took Fr. Ted out for lunch." This was our first contact with an Orthodox Christian and the beginning of a strong, lasting friendship.

Two important steps forward were taken in 1977. First, Ken Berven launched our publishing arm, Conciliar Press, and began the quarterly magazine, *Again*. This established an immediate and effective point of contact both with evangelical and Orthodox Christians. Secondly, we started the Academy of Orthodox Theology in Santa Barbara (later named for Saint Athanasius) for the purpose of grouping together a community of scholars to research the Orthodox Faith, to do translation work, and to train our young people. We invited Bishop Dmitri to speak to our students during his visit to Santa Barbara in 1978.

Earlier in 1978, a group of us had driven down to Saint Innocent Orthodox Church in Tarzana for a Holy Week service. We saw in action at Saint Innocent's everything we had read about. But culturally the service seemed worlds removed from us. By the time the Bishop arrived we were overflowing with more questions.

"Why do they pray, 'Lord, have mercy' so often?"

"Tell us about the priest's vestments."

"What do all the candles on that stand mean?"

"Is there incense at every service?"

Being familiar with evangelical Protestantism himself,

the Bishop understood our culture shock. We believed the basic doctrines of this ancient faith, but the rubrics, or detailed explanations of how to actually conduct a liturgical service, simply were not in the history books.

"Let's start with our faith in Christ," advised Bishop Dmitri. "We must be sure we're in agreement on the question asked by the Lord Himself: 'Who do men say that I am?' If we're together on Him as begotten of the Father from all eternity, incarnate in the womb of Mary, and as the Savior of our souls, everything else in Orthodox Christianity will fall into place. Because everything we do relates specifically to Christ—vestments, prayers, icons, all of it."

We talked through the doctrine of Christ, and we did agree. Emphatically! From the doctrine of the Incarnation, we worked our way out to other things surrounding it. And piece by piece, truth by truth, a picture of the whole began taking shape.

In 1978, several of us had the opportunity to visit Saint Vladimir's Seminary in New York. Still brimming with questions and learning the protocol (my, are they patient out there!), we were warmly welcomed by Metropolitan Theodosius, the head of the OCA, and Professors Alexander Schmemann, John Meyendorff, Thomas Hopko, Paul Lazar, and Veselin Kesich. Many of these men also came to teach periodically at Saint Athanasius, Santa Barbara. Wonderful conversations full of inspiration, instruction, and laughter could be recounted with each of these brethren. But let me single out just one of them: that champion for Christ, Fr. Alexander Schmemann.

He was a statesman in the Kingdom of God (really, the *was* could be *is;* he went to be with the Lord in 1983). A lump forms in my throat as I write about this man of such blessed memory. Speaking humanly, if you could say a person "led us to the Church" (as one would say so-and-so "led me to Christ"), Fr. Alexander was pivotal in leading us into the twentieth–century Orthodox Church.

On three occasions he traveled west to be with us in Santa Barbara. By the time he came for his first visit later in 1978, we were at the point in our tracing of the Church where we sided with the East in 1054. We were doctrinally on our way to being Orthodox. We had it in our heads, somewhat in our hearts, but we practiced very little of it liturgically. Our sanctuary, for example, was little more than four bare walls and a pulpit.

Somehow, Fr. Alexander was not put off by our lack of externals and was able to see through to our heads and hearts. It was, mutually, love at first sight. He told his wife, Julianna, after the trip, "They're Orthodox, but they don't really know it yet."

While he was in Santa Barbara, we naturally asked for his guidance. As we look back, he was very careful not to give us too much to do or teach us more than we could handle. "It would help if you were to construct an altar and put up a few icons," he advised.

By his next visit, in early 1981, we had built an altar, and beside it on the wall, one on each side, were two small icons—a bit larger than postcard sized—one of Christ, the other of the Virgin Mary. With great pride in our astounding progress, I took Father into the sanctuary and up toward the altar. He finally got close enough to squint and see our iconic adornments. He smiled, "Well, I can go home and finally report that you people are no longer in active opposition to icons!" On some days, he absolutely kidded us into being Orthodox.

It was on this second visit that he gave us another point of direction which turned out to be pivotal to the rest of our journey. Speaking to our synod concerning the various Orthodox jurisdictions in North America, he advised us,

"Don't get to know just the OCA. When it comes time for you to enter Orthodoxy, you will be joining the *whole* Church. So get to know the Greeks, the Antiochians, the Serbians."

Enlarging the Circle of Friendship

About this same time, one of our presbyters in the Midwest met a Greek Orthodox priest, Fr. James Carrellas, who, he reported, "preaches just like an evangelical." On my next trip to that area, a meeting was arranged with Fr. Jim. I know it's not the only indicator, but when you talk with a fellow pastor about Jesus Christ and tears well up in his eyes, you suspect you've found a true soul-brother.

"One man you've got to meet is Bishop Maximos of Pittsburgh," Fr. Jim told me after he had heard our story. "This man has a real vision for Orthodoxy in America and loves converts who come in from the outside." I was to be in Pittsburgh in two months, so I made a mental note and later phoned ahead for an appointment.

The phrase I always use to describe Bishop Maximos is "Christ-centered," a term he often uses himself. I tell people he's half human and half angel. As we talked in his beautiful turn-of-the-century residence on Ellsworth Avenue in Pittsburgh, he asked if I could return to the city and speak to the college students in his diocese about my commitment to Christ and the Church.

That college meeting several months later was one of the spiritual highlights of my life. Some two hundred life-long Orthodox students came to hear of our journey. A number of students told me afterwards that they had committed themselves to the Lord in a new way that evening. One young man who had just returned to town after trekking around the country for two months remarked, "Father, you gave me the kick in the butt I needed tonight!"

Two other memories of that same trip stand out in my mind. The next evening I spoke to a group of laypeople at Saint Nicholas Cathedral. After my remarks, there were questions and answers. One lady said, "I can't believe you think we should worship and receive communion each week. My grandmother taught me we're not worthy to do that more than once or twice a year."

"If it were a matter of our own worthiness, we could never come to Christ," I answered. "Because of our union with Him, He has set us on the road to being made new. Therefore, we are by His grace and His mercy called to an entire life of communion with Him."

Just as I said, "Perhaps His Grace would like to comment on this," I could see out of the corner of my eye that the Bishop was already on the way to the podium. As he exhorted his flock to deeper commitment to Christ, I could see that besides loving God he also hated minimalism. I actually checked the lectern when the meeting adjourned to see if it had cracked when his clenched fist struck it twice during his exhortation. (I'd like to think I saw at least a little hairline separation in the grain of the wood!)

The following day, I was back at his residence teaching a portion of the Book of Romans to a group of lay leaders and clergy. Someone interrupted during the session to say that as Orthodox, everything we needed to hear was in the Liturgy, and we didn't need to know the Bible. This time I didn't have a chance to respond. The Bishop was on his feet to set the matter straight, starting out in English and finishing up in Greek! I don't know all of what he said, but as in New Testament times, the inquisitor "durst ask no more questions!"

The fact is that in any group, political or primeval,

Baptist or Byzantine, you've got those who are hot and those who are lukewarm. Under the leadership of "Bishop Max," the diocese of Pittsburgh has experienced wonderful renewal. I've learned from him how to encourage people toward love and good works.

Our next contact with the Greek Orthodox Archdiocese came the following year at Holy Cross Seminary in Boston. A group of us had been invited to dialogue with the faculty. Fr. Alkiviadis Calivas, dean, hosted the meetings which included Fathers Stanley Harakas, Ted Stylianopoulos, Tom Fitzgerald (there's a convert!), George Papademitriou, and Michael Vaporis—as well as a number of Boston-area priests. Before our second visit to Holy Cross, I met and visited with Archbishop Iakovos in New York and his gracious assistant, the late Fr. Alexander Doumouros.

I cannot say enough about the gracious hospitality extended to us during both of our visits to Holy Cross. The faculty emulates that winning combination of careful Orthodox scholarship and genuine spiritual warmth. Bishop Maximos was with us on both of these visits. In conjunction with our dialogue, I was asked to deliver the Saint John Chrysostom lecture series on biblical preaching during our 1983 visit. Everyone at Holy Cross seemed encouraged by the presence of two-thousand evangelical "Bible-believers" heading toward Orthodox Christianity.

During this same period of time, I was doing my best to arrange an appointment with a man so many spoke of so highly, Metropolitan Philip Saliba, head of the Antiochian Orthodox Church in North America. In fact, someone at Holy Cross had made a prediction that after all was said and done, the door through which we would enter Orthodoxy would be that of Antioch. On at least three occasions, when I was in New York, Metropolitan Philip was somewhere else. We could not get our schedules to mesh.

Byzantine Intrigue

Our courtship with the Orthodox Church was well on its way. But in any courtship, there are two ways for things to go wrong. One, you can plan the wedding too soon, without giving the couple adequate time to get to know each other. We were sure that if we were to err, it would not be in that direction. The other mistake, of course, is waiting too long. In this second scenario, the courtship drags out so long you risk falling out of love.

In January of 1985, we met as the Synod of the Evangelical Orthodox Church. Fr. Gordon Walker felt that to wait much longer to make a specific move toward entrance into the Orthodox Church would be to risk falling away. "Let me make a proposal," he began. "I believe we should call Bishop Maximos from right here at this conference center and ask him to arrange to take us to Constantinople (modern-day Istanbul). With so many Orthodox jurisdictions in America, I believe we need to present ourselves directly to the Ecumenical Patriarch and seek his guidance as to how we should enter the Church. Surely as Ecumenical Patriarch, he can give us specific instructions instead of us trying to decide on our own what to do."

After a fairly brief discussion, everyone agreed this was the course to take. I looked at my watch. We were in California, and Pittsburgh was three hours later. "It's too late to call," I said. "I'll phone Bishop Max in the morning." Just then Tom Webster walked in the room and handed me a note: *Marilyn called. Bishop Maximos is trying to reach Fr. Gordon. Please have him return the call.* "Thank you, Lord," I whispered under my breath.

"Good morning, Your Grace," Fr. Gordon said the next morning at 7:00, with me on the extension. "I understand you called. And I think we have some news you'll want to hear." Bishop Max had called to invite Fr. Gordon to speak at a renewal conference, and he was overjoyed with our decision concerning Constantinople. He set out to begin making arrangements through the Archdiocesan offices in New York.

"Those dates are perfect. If we go in early June, we can spend the afternoon of Pentecost on the Island of Halki where I went to seminary. That day will be the seventh anniversary of my elevation to the Episcopacy," said Bishop Maximos. "There is no place I would rather be in all the world on Pentecost Sunday."

The nineteen of us who served as bishops in the EOC returned home from the synod meeting to begin at once getting passports and passing the hat for airfare, lodging expenses, and a cash gift to the Patriarch. Further, each man would bring a particular gift that was representative of his part of North America—Eskimo craft-work from Alaska, a box of fruit from the Northwest, a coffee-table picture-book from Nashville.

In April, 1985, we had a visit from John Bartke, by now a priest assigned as pastor to Saint Michael Antiochian Orthodox Church in Van Nuys, California. "We just got word that the Patriarch of Antioch, Ignatius IV, will be here in L.A. in late June or early July. Metropolitan Philip will be with him. I'd like to set up an appointment for you men to see them," he informed us.

I wasn't sure just how to respond. On the one hand, I had tried repeatedly to see Metropolitan Philip, and here was an opportunity to meet the Patriarch as well. But on the other hand, we were committed to go to Constantinople, and I didn't want it to appear we were playing both ends against the middle, looking for "the best deal."

As I was weighing my words, Fr. John interrupted. "Look, I know you're on the way to see the Ecumenical

Patriarch, and it may well be he will give you the direction you seek in entering the Church. If nothing else, bring a few of the men with you and come meet our Patriarch and the Metropolitan out of honor. After all, it will still be important for you to meet the leaders of the Antiochian Church."

"You're absolutely right," I said. "Schedule us in and let me know the date and place."

In May, Marilyn and I planned a four-day, twenty-fifth anniversary trip to New York. "I've got one 'business call' I'd like to make," I told her. "But I won't schedule it unless you tell me I can."

"What is it?" she asked, knowing our time there was brief.

"I'd like us to stop by and see Archbishop Iakovos to ask his blessing on our trip to Constantinople."

"I'd love to meet him," she said.

I called his appointment secretary, and he was booked. But a call came back the next day saying he had moved an appointment and would see us at noon on the Friday we were there. He had already given his approval for Bishop Maximos to lead our delegation to the Patriarchate, but somehow I wanted to let him know personally of our sincerity in going.

On the appointed Friday in May we arrived at the Greek Orthodox Archdiocesan Headquarters in New York, only to learn that the Archbishop had gone home that morning with the flu. We had a cordial visit with some of the other hierarchs and left a gift for Archbishop Iakovos and a note wishing his speedy recovery. We took the train to Crestwood for Friday evening Vespers at Saint Vladimir's and spent the rest of the weekend celebrating twenty-five great years of marriage.

I was at home on the morning before the day of departure for Constantinople, helping feed our children breakfast. The phone rang. It was Bishop Maximos. His voice was that of a deeply disappointed man. "I don't know what has happened," he said, "but the Archbishop does not want me to go. I'm recommending that Father Gregory Wingenbach accompany you in my place."

When Orthodox people joke about such sudden changes, they call it Byzantine Intrigue. This is when unexpected things happen at the highest levels of the Church, and nobody seems to know the reason why. It was all new to us. And the joke was not funny.

I phoned Fr. Gregory, who had been a close friend for years, and he was puzzled as well. "The Lord's hand is still in this thing," he assured me. "The Bishop is sick about missing his anniversary at Halki with us, but he promised to call us on Sunday night at the hotel. I'll meet those of you who are flying through New York at JFK tomorrow night."

I reminded myself that when you're an Archbishop, you do get to change your mind.

The Pilgrimage to Constantinople

The next day all of us who were making the trip together from Santa Barbara hopped in a rental car and headed down the 101 and the 405 toward Los Angeles International Airport (LAX). Along with Fr. Wingenbach, we would meet the other EOC bishops from the Eastern U.S. in London, spend the night, and fly together to Constantinople the next day.

What I didn't know until returning home two weeks later was that Archbishop Iakovos had sent me a last-minute telegram, notifying me we "should not go at this time." The telegram arrived after we were already in the air flying across the arctic from LAX to London.

We have since been told that a few Greek Orthodox clergy along with a Greek government official were adamantly opposed to our going to Constantinople and our entering the Church. They reportedly felt we would somehow "water down" Orthodoxy in America to a pop version of the ancient faith and not be supportive of retaining a commitment to hellenistic culture in the parishes. One report suggested we were out to "take over the Church."

Most of our delegation learned en route to New York or London that Bishop Maximos was not on the trip and that it was possible we would not be received by the Patriarch. My feeling was, if we fail in our mission, at least let's do it boldly. We simply kept on hoping that things would work out.

Then, there was one more surprise. We were arriving in Constantinople during Ramadan, a time when many Muslims fast all day and stay up all night to eat, drink, and make noise! Then, somewhere around 3:00 A.M. they pray and make even more noise. In June it is so hot you keep the windows open all night long unless your hotel has air conditioning. Since we were in one of the oldest hotels in the "historic" section of that ancient city, and since the toilets emitted foul odors, we had little choice. In Constantinople you can either close the windows and not sleep because of the heat and odor, or open them and not sleep due to the noise. Some nights it is so hot you can have it both ways!

Joining us in Constantinople was one other key person, my neighbor, Dr. Apostolos Athanassakis, chairman of the Department of Classics at the University of California, Santa Barbara. He was spending a year at the University of Crete and flew up to Constantinople to meet us. He had close personal friends in both the government of Turkey and at the Patriarchate. In addition he was a brilliant and diplomatically sensitive interpreter for us. His help was incalculable.

The Sunday of Pentecost came two days after our arrival. We arose early and took a chartered bus to the Patriarchate and worshiped on this great feastday in the Church of Saint George. The Ecumenical Patriarch, Demetrios, was there with his synod of Metropolitans on each side of him. The twenty or so of us stood across from him, either in hand-carved wooden stalls, or on the stone floor. The normally lengthy liturgy was made even longer by the beautiful Pentecostal Prayers of Kneeling. Fr. Gregory Wingenbach had an English translation of the service and kept passing it around to us as we knelt together on the stone floor of the Church.

After the Liturgy, we received the *antidoran*—the blessed bread—from the Patriarch. Fr. Gregory quickly explained in Greek who we were. By now the Patriarch had already been fully informed about us. Though we knew it was highly unlikely that our whole group could have the dialogue with him that we had come for, we expected at the least a brief courtesy visit. But no such visit materialized.

Instead the Patriarch and his synod of Metropolitans exited the Church, leaving us standing alone. Fr. Gordon Walker exploded. "Where are they going?" he asked Fr. Gregory. "Do you mean we have spent fifty thousand dollars and traveled thousands of miles to have them turn and walk away? If we were Muslims they would treat us with greater dignity than this! Fr. Gregory, ask them to come back and at least speak with us!"

Fr. Gregory immediately started after them and engaged some of the Metropolitans in a lively discussion. A few moments later Metropolitans Chrysostomos and Bartholomeou, who became Ecumenical Patriarch in 1991, graciously came back to speak with us. They greeted us in the name of the Patriarch but stated that no dialogue or any sort of meeting could be held with him. They admonished us to return home and continue our dialogue there.

After a brief picture-taking session before the iconostasis of Saint George Church we headed back to the bus. On board we erupted in heated debate and discussion. Fr. Gregory, while remaining loyal to his hierarchs, tried to console us in our disappointment and frustration and help us understand what was happening.

That afternoon the tour company that had arranged our trip had engaged a private ferry to take us up the Bosporus River to the Black Sea and back. Hardly anyone wanted to go. We were too downcast to enjoy the trip. But our refusal would offend the local people who had planned the trip, so we went on with it. It was a good time to soothe our injured feelings.

That Sunday night at the hotel we held a meeting in the penthouse room which had been provided for our synod sessions. The room was spacious and had glass walls on four sides which allowed a 360-degree panorama of old Constantinople. Our memories are etched with the sad but beautiful sight of innumerable domes of Churches long ago closed by the Turks. What a city and culture it once must have been.

In our synod meeting that night we decided to make a last-ditch effort to see the Patriarch or at least his representatives in an official meeting. We asked Dr. Athanassakis (his last name means "little Athanasius") to write an appeal to the Patriarch on our behalf and to personally deliver it to him. Some of us worked for hours with him as he first composed a beautiful letter in English and then translated it into polished Greek.

On Monday morning he went to the Patriarchate only to be told the two Metropolitans, Chrysostomos and

Bartholomeou, were serving the Pentecost Liturgy in sub-
urbs some distance away. He spent all day taking cabs
to the Churches and personally appealing to these men.
In response, they invited us to send representatives to the
Patriarchate the next day, Tuesday, for a meeting.

In the meantime the rest of us took a huge ferry to the
island of Halki to visit the seminary which Bishop
Maximos attended and which had been closed by the
Turks years before. We rode in horse-drawn carriages
from the sea landing to the school and I'll always remember the beautiful view of the bay from the seminary
at the top of the hill. But we will remember even more
the loving reception given us by the late Metropolitan
Maximos, a godly man who lived out his days there,
basically alone. The incredibly beautiful seminary, with
its incomparable library containing ancient volumes in
uncial Greek, was under Turkish domination and at that
time not available for use by the Church.

On Tuesday morning I selected Richard Ballew, who
was serving as the Western Archdiocesan Bishop of the
EOC, and Gordon Walker, who was serving as Eastern
Archdiocesan Bishop, to go with me to the Patriarchate. We
took along Tom Webster and Marc Dunaway to help carry
the many heavy suitcases of gifts and to take pictures. As
interpreter and liaison, Dr. Athanassakis and Fr. Gregory
Wingenbach accompanied us as well.

Dr. Athanassakis had done his work thoroughly. The
one-hour meeting with Metropolitans Chrysostomos and
Bartholomeou was cordial and warm. We showed them
pictures of our people and presented our gifts, which
included a $3,000 check. The Metropolitans said the
money would be used for an orphanage near Constantinople. But the end result was the same as on Sunday. No
substantial direction or help for entering the Orthodox

Church was given to us.

All that was left to do was to make some sightseeing trips around Constantinople and the surrounding area, including stops at the awe-inspiring Hagia Sophia and the Blue Mosque. At the close of our visit we flew to Thessalonica, Greece and from there to Athens before flying back home.

Holy Cross Revisited

We landed in Boston, instead of New York, by design. At the gracious invitation of the faculty, we had decided to return to Holy Cross Seminary for the meeting of our synod—supposedly to discuss the direction received from Constantinople and to decide together what to do in response. But there was nothing to respond to.

We gathered in the board room at the Seminary the morning after our arrival in Boston. I have never been more grateful in my life that a meeting was not preserved by tape recording. It was the closest we ever came to collectively turning back from the Orthodox Church. But to forsake the Church, you must also forsake the faith, and we could not do that. We knew too much. Besides, there was no place else to go.

As we left the administration building later that day in varying degrees of despair, we looked up and there was Bishop Maximos! Like Christ Himself, he would neither leave us nor forsake us. He joined us for dinner that night and reminded us to keep on seeking to do God's will. God grant you many years, Your Grace!

The flight from Boston's Logan Field to our various cities of destination was very quiet for all of us. I can personally testify that it was extremely sullen for those of us flying into Los Angeles. Here was the end to the most spectacular trip any of us had ever taken. The ancient Churches were magnificent. At Thessalonica we gathered and prayed, each one of us, at the place Saint Paul stood and preached when he first came to that city. I rededicated my life to Christ and to the preaching of His Gospel that day, with a wonderful sense of God's presence.

On another day we sang the Trisagion hymn together, crying our eyes out with joy, before the altar area of the oldest known existing church building in Christendom, just outside Constantinople. Christians had sung that hymn there for hundreds and hundreds of years. Some of the other tourists wept, too, and I'm not even sure they understood why.

The whole trip was like that, one spiritual high after another. But it was still a colossal disappointment. We had knocked on the door of Orthodoxy so hard our knuckles were red. There were discussions, nods, and pleasantries, but not one invitation to enter the fold. Or as they say in the West, there was no cigar.

Back home, even sunny Santa Barbara looked gray.

11

WELCOME HOME!

"Wait a minute!" I said. Jon Braun, Richard Ballew, and I were sitting with Jack Sparks on the patio behind his house on Sunday afternoon, two days after the Constantinople-Boston trip, still recovering from jet lag. "Do you remember that in three days we've got an appointment to see the Patriarch of Antioch?"

"At least we won't have to go halfway across the world to keep it," somebody muttered.

"I'd forgotten all about that," one of the others said.

The anticipation gave us just enough encouragement to let us drag ourselves through the remainder of that day. And the next, and the next.

It was Wednesday when Bishop Braun, Bishop Ballew, and I were on our way in the morning sun to Los Angeles. Jack Sparks had stayed home with his now persistent bad back.

"You know what I think we should do today?" Jon Braun asked. "I think we should have fun!"

"What on earth are you talking about?" I asked. The two of us, Bishop Richard and I, waited for the worst philosophical discussion we would hear all week.

"We went to Constantinople all serious, worried about how to greet everybody, when to stand, when to sit down. Today, let's just be ourselves and enjoy it."

Neither Bishop Richard nor I could bring ourselves to say anything. "Let him drone on," I thought to myself.

He did.

"I mean, here's what I'm going to do. I'm going to say to Metropolitan Philip, 'Your Eminence, it's *great* to meet you,' and I'm really going to mean it. I'm not going to act religious, or pompous, or pious." ("If that were even possible," I whispered inaudibly.) "I'm just going to walk in there and be enthusiastic, and if the Patriarch and the Metropolitan like our program, fine. And if they don't, well that's just fine, too. Then we'll find ourselves another Patriarch and another Metropolitan somewhere else. But I'll tell you what. I'm tired of all the pressure. I'm just going to enjoy myself and have some fun."

By now, the two of us were beginning to catch his spirit. We knew we had to shake the gloom cloud of Constantinople. It would be an insult both to these hierarchs and to those we represented in the EOC to simply walk in hat in hand. It was time to shake the blues and go for it. And one more thing. We agreed to avoid getting into a dump session if asked about Constantinople. After all, we still did not know why things fell apart. We would report what we knew: it did not work out. We would avoid speculation or assigning blame.

Just inside the big glass front door of the Sheraton Universal Hotel we met Dr. Fred Milkie who had been assigned to watch for us and take us up to the Patriarch's quarters on the seventh floor. Dr. Milkie is a tall, engaging man with a warm smile—exactly what we needed to set our appointment on the joyful note we were after. Through the lobby, on the elevator, off on the seventh floor, down the hall, and to the end we went. Fred knocked on the door.

Meeting the Antiochians

One of the deacons answered and invited us in. Metropolitan Philip stepped up to greet us. "What a pleasure after so long a time," he said with a firm handshake and wonderful eye contact. He seemed so very genuine; there was no air at all of his being professionally hierarchical. It was as though I was meeting an extremely distinguished Christian executive. He had a warm and very caring presence about him. "Come, let me introduce you to our Patriarch, Ignatius."

At the opposite end of the large central room, just next to the window, sat the Patriarch of Antioch. Every now and then you meet a person who immediately strikes you as *looking* like a Christian. This was my distinct impression of him. His face was saintly—and joyful. As we approached him, he extended his arms to us and smiled. "Brothers, welcome," he said.

Could it be possible that we three prodigals had just found home?

We talked for close to an hour, the five of us—the Patriarch, the Metropolitan, Jon Braun, Richard Ballew, and I. We were asked to tell about the process of our coming to embrace Orthodox Christianity, about our families, and about our recent journey overseas. We reviewed for them something about each of the parishes within the Evangelical Orthodox Church and described our service agencies—Saint Athanasius College, Conciliar Press, and our campus outreach.

After three-quarters of an hour, Metropolitan Philip turned to Patriarch Ignatius for his assessment. "Let us do everything we can to help them," the Patriarch responded.

"All right," the Metropolitan said turning back to us. "You will find out something about this Archdiocese. We make decisions, and we make them quickly."

This was the best news I had heard in months!

"I would like you to supply me with two things. First, I would like a brief history of the Evangelical Orthodox Church, going through your journey to Orthodoxy step by step. Then, secondly, prepare for me a profile of each parish—who the pastor is, his education, the number of people, the facilities—not more than a page for each one."

"I'd like to volunteer to do that," Jon Braun said.

"When can you have it to me?"

"Let's see, it's the end of June," said Bishop Jon. "What about Labor Day?"

"That will be fine. Mail it to my office in Englewood. And send with it copies of your *Again* Magazine, the books and other literature that the EOC has produced, and things that have been written about you. We will review this thoroughly and get back to you."

We stood up to say goodbye. The Metropolitan shook my hand firmly and once again looked me straight in the eye. "We will not keep you waiting long," he said.

I think all three of us made the same silent wish that nobody else would be on the elevator so we could press the "Lobby" button, watch the door slide to a close, and *shout!*

"Where have these men been all our lives?" I yelled with glee.

We were too excited to get in the car and drive home. We were too light-headed to go anywhere. So we walked down a flight of stairs to the coffee shop and ordered lunch. I remember nothing else at all that was said the rest of the day.

The report and two boxes of literature were mailed just

prior to Labor Day, and in late fall I was again in touch with the Metropolitan's office. The EOC Synod of Bishops was to meet in mid-January, 1986, and Metropolitan Philip requested that we draft a proposal as to how we would foresee being made a part of the Church: a suggested time frame, how we would see the integration of our parishes and agencies into the Archdiocese, and problems we might anticipate. Our January Synod deliberations produced a very specific two and one-half page proposal. We set a date in early March 1986 for me to go to Englewood and discuss that proposal.

Defining the Specifics

As March approached, I was asked to attend a meeting of the National Association of Evangelicals (NAE) in Kansas City. It worked out for me to schedule that meeting and then fly directly on to Newark for my discussions with Metropolitan Philip.

On the second day of the NAE meeting I was given a message to call my secretary at our church office in Santa Barbara. "Metropolitan Philip's secretary, Kathy Meyer, called you this morning," Linda Wallace said. "He and his staff have completed the final reading of all those materials we sent, and he wants to meet with you the whole day tomorrow, not just an hour or two. They want you to fly in tonight."

"I can do it," I said, "but I'll need you to re-schedule the flight, get me a hotel room, and call back. We're in meetings all day here."

"You won't need a hotel reservation," Linda said. "He has asked that you stay at his residence."

When Linda phoned back with the flight information she had already called Kathy Meyer with the 10:00 P.M.

arrival time. "The Metropolitan's assistant is Deacon Hans, and he will meet you at the gate. Kathy said you will spot him easily because he looks just like Omar Sharif!"

Archdeacon Hans is one of the most gracious men I have ever met, and everyone else who knows him says the same thing. He is an icon of Christian servanthood, a celibate in his middle years, a native of Lebanon, and a graduate of Saint Vladimir's Seminary. And he does look just like Omar Sharif.

It was after 11:00 P.M. by the time we reached Englewood. The residence which serves as both the Metropolitan's home and his archdiocesan headquarters is a large, traditional Tudor structure in a suburban community of New York City. The house was quiet when we tiptoed through the front door and headed upstairs with the luggage to my room. The deacon followed me into the room with my suitcase. I laid my briefcase on a chair and hooked my hanging bag on the back of the bathroom door. I said thank you and good night to Deacon Hans as I walked him to the door, and here, down the hall, came Metropolitan Philip in his robe. He had gotten up to welcome me to his home.

"Bishop Peter, it's an honor to have you here," he said as he ignored my outstretched hand and opened his arms for an embrace. "The Lord has given you a safe trip. You get some rest, and we will meet downstairs at 10:00 in the morning."

Fr. Paul Schneirla, pastor of Saint Mary's Orthodox Church in Brooklyn, would join us for the morning meeting. He arrived early and the two of us had breakfast together. Fr. Paul is a former Lutheran pastor who converted to Orthodoxy over forty-five years ago and has brought many others into the Orthodox Church.

Just before 10:00, Metropolitan Philip came downstairs

with a paper in his hand. "Good morning," he said. "I'm ready to meet. I asked you to bring a proposal, and I have one, too." He handed me a copy of his, and I gave him ours. We stood in the front hall outside his office, each skimming the other's paper.

"I see we're on the same track," he said. His single-paged proposal had nine points which in content matched very closely what we had written. "Let's go into the dining room where we can sit and talk around the table. Kathy will bring us some coffee."

The dining room at the back of the house was a recent addition and the size of a small banquet room (numerous dinners and meetings are hosted there each year). The back wall had glass panels and a sliding glass door which opened out on a spacious slate patio. This was surrounded by a large lawn area and countless trees. The long table on the left-hand side of the room had three note pads and pencils set out at the far end.

The day was spent in conversation, primarily over our proposals. Since Metropolitan Philip's was the briefer of the two, we used it as the working paper and incorporated a few of our points into it. We finished the day with the following document, with which the three of us stood in full agreement:

PRELIMINARY AGREEMENT BETWEEN
METROPOLITAN PHILIP AND
BISHOP PETER GILLQUIST

1. Expression of hope for full union in the near future.

2. The union will require some modifications of attitudes on both sides. It will be necessary for us to solve the problem of a married episcopate. This will be worked through at a future

meeting between the Metropolitan and the Synod of the Evangelical Orthodox Church.

3. Upon the chrismation and/or ordination of those who are willing and meet the requirements, a relationship can be set up bringing the Evangelical Orthodox Church into the Antiochian Archdiocese.

4. The structure that is now the Evangelical Orthodox Church will continue its mission of preaching Orthodoxy to the American public.

5. Under the Metropolitan, the new body will be headed by a Council under its president.

6. The Metropolitan will appoint an acceptable liaison officer to work with the headquarters of what is now the Evangelical Orthodox Church. The officer will advise and answer questions that the Council may have and after a given period, his office will be closed.

7. A committee of theologians to whom the Council can refer theological and liturgical problems will be appointed by the Metropolitan.

8. The new structure will follow the financial system now enforced in the Archdiocese and will report quarterly to the Archdiocese on its financial status and growth or decline.

9. The new structure in the Archdiocese will establish internal liturgical uniformity acceptable to all in consultation with the Committee of Theologians.

I would present this paper to the EOC Synod in June for

discussion and response. We broke for lunch and adjourned after the meal to the living room to finish up.

"I would like to make an important request of you, Your Eminence," I said as we sat down. "Our men should be able to agree to what we have written this morning. But if we are talking about entrance into the Antiochian Archdiocese, it will be crucial that all nineteen of us have an opportunity to meet you soon to hear your vision for bringing Orthodoxy to North America and to interact with you face to face on some of these items. Is it possible that after our June Synod, say at the end of the summer, we could come here and spend a day with you?"

"Absolutely," he said without hesitation. "Let's look at early September."

Our Synod in June was not nineteen, but fifteen. Four of our bishops elected to step away from the EOC. Their desire was to cease in any effort to be received into the Orthodox Church, and to get on with building the EOC. We urged them to wait with their decision until September, 1986, when at least they would have the opportunity to converse with the Metropolitan, whom they had never met. But that was not to be. Had the Constantinople disappointment helped to take this toll? No one could tell, but we could not convince them to come.

September arrived and here we were, the Synod of the EOC, on the plane again, this time to New York. We came into town on a Thursday night with fifteen bishops and another fifteen observers. We rented cars and drove to a motel just outside Englewood. The schedule called for us to meet all day Friday with Metropolitan Philip. On Saturday morning we would gather at Saint Anthony's Church in nearby Bergenfield, New Jersey, to celebrate the Divine Liturgy before the Metropolitan for his evaluation and assessment. On Sunday we would worship together at

Saint Anthony's and then drive across the George Washington Bridge to Crestwood. There the Synod would meet in the afternoon at Saint Vladimir's Seminary. We would stay there for several days to reach a decision on entering the Church.

Meeting the Metropolitan

The mood as we entered the Friday morning meeting with Metropolitan Philip was sober. A number of the men were ready to be Orthodox. Others were still somewhat hesitant, expressing the concern of being "swallowed up"—the same fear which had kept the other men out.

Friday morning we met around the same long table where the three of us had sat together back in March. Note pads and pencils were again in place, this time two dozen of them. With the Metropolitan at his end of the table was His Eminence, Metropolitan Constantine of Bagdad, who had been visiting that week, His Grace Bishop Antoun, auxiliary to the Metropolitan, and Fr. Joseph Allen, vicar-general of the Antiochian Archdiocese in North America. The observers sat just behind us. Kathy Meyer and Deacon Hans kept us all supplied with coffee.

Metropolitan Philip opened the meeting with prayer and a prepared statement, which included these remarks:

> We are aware to a certain extent of your background and your quest to fully embrace the Holy Orthodox faith. We are also aware that your journey toward Orthodoxy has not been an easy one, due to the multiplicity of Orthodox jurisdictions on this continent. I am sure, however, that the Holy Spirit which is always present in the Church shall, in the words of the Pentecost service, "lead you into the right land." Orthodoxy, despite its jurisdictional situation in North America, is

still Christ's eternal truth yesterday, today, and forever.

I would like to caution you not to make hasty decisions; at the same time, my brotherly advice to you is not to procrastinate for the rest of your days. Whatever decision you make, now or in the future, make it together in one mind, one heart, and one spirit. Do not permit Satan, who is the master of deceit and dissension, to enter into your midst and destroy your unity. God knows we have enough splinter religious groups in this country, and we have enough spiritual blindness.

We do admire your evangelical zeal and we are deeply convinced that our Lord did not die on the cross and raise from the dead to establish his Church for Slavs, Greeks, and Arabs, but for all mankind. In Him East and West, North and South, do not exist. "Go ye therefore, and make disciples of all nations, baptizing them in the name of the Father, and of the Son, and of the Holy Spirit."

It is in this spirit that we welcome you again to your home. May the All-Holy Spirit lead all of us to do what is pleasing to His holy Church.

By day's end we had quite thoroughly gone through the proposal paper, with the Metropolitan and the others graciously and patiently answering our questions. Most of the observers took part in the exchange. The Liturgy and discussion on Saturday were beneficial as well, for we had learned Orthodox worship "out of the books," and several adjustments were needed. The people at Saint Anthony's welcomed us Sunday with a delicious and massive spread of food after the Divine Liturgy.

Now our courtship had reached a new level. The ball was clearly in our court. We had studied Orthodox Christianity for fifteen years and interacted with its people for a decade. The Metropolitan had given us more time than we had asked for, answered every question we put forth, and offered to be our father in Christ. He would bring us into the Church within a year if we were ready to make the commitment. We drove back to Saint Vladimir's and settled in for the night. The most important meeting of our lives was set for Monday morning at 9:00 A.M. I remember it distinctly.

After an opening prayer I said, "Brethren, I have never run a meeting like this in my life, nor have I ever attended one. Therefore, I am simply going to sit down, and you may speak as you wish."

Harold Dunaway was the first man to speak. From the Constantinople trip on, he had developed a growing hesitance over entering the Church. I predicted he would be negative. "Gentlemen, we have no choice," he said. "I say yes. I'm ready to go in." He is a man of few words, and this may have been one of his longer speeches!

Next, Weldon Hardenbrook spoke up. He, too, had been negative in the last year, in much the same frame of mind as Harold. "I'm in," he said. "I liked what I saw this weekend."

With these two men affirmative, that was it. Everyone knew it. In five minutes, or less, the meeting was over, except for the formality of the others saying yes. There was one "maybe" who wanted more time, and in the weeks ahead he evolved to a "no." But even he felt we should enter the Church. We were fourteen strong on the Synod, with seventeen parishes and nearly two thousand people from Alaska to Atlanta.

I want to say it was the happiest day of my life, but that day was yet to come. I was happy to be sure. But that part of me which manufactures feelings had been on overload all weekend, and the magnitude of what had just happened was blunted. We adjourned the morning session before noon, and I meant to go to the phone to call Metropolitan Philip. But I ran into a friend on the Saint Vladimir's faculty and never made the call. By the time we finished lunch, it was time to reconvene.

We recessed for the day just before 4:00 and I left the room quickly to call Englewood. Kathy Meyer answered. "I have some good news for the Metropolitan if he's in," I said.

"Bishop Peter, thank you for calling," he said as he picked up the phone.

"I am thrilled to report to you that our answer is yes," I said, "but we would like to tell you in person. If we showed up at 3:00 Wednesday afternoon, would you come out on the steps of the house and give us a blessing? I have in mind five minutes at the most."

"Kathy, am I here at three on Wednesday?" I heard him ask away from the phone. Something was mumbled from the other room about having to leave a meeting.

"I'll be here and will be happy to see you. Come at three."

The next morning I told the men as we began the meeting that we had to promise each other to make it brief on Wednesday. "He's interrupting something to see us," I said. "Let's show up right on time, I'll say yes on behalf of all of us, we'll ask for his blessing, and take off."

We met together over EOC business all day Tuesday and again on Wednesday morning. After lunch Wednesday we jumped in our cars and drove the 40 minutes to Englewood. At 2:55 the last car pulled up to the curb. We met for a moment in the driveway. "Let's go together down the walk to the front steps. Deacon Howard Shannon will knock on the door and I'll take it from there. Remember, five minutes max."

Down the walk we went, and we stood together at the

foot of the steps. Deacon Howard knocked and Archdeacon Hans came to the door, followed by the Metropolitan. "Come in," motioned Metropolitan Philip.

"Your Eminence, thank you, but you're busy and all we want is to tell you our decision and ask for your. . . ."

"I said come in," he interrupted, maybe just a bit perturbed. "Hans, bring them in here. Come on, come on."

He headed for the banquet room at the back, and we reluctantly followed. I looked up and could not believe my eyes. The tables were arranged in a U shape across the front of the room and down both sides. They were covered with linen, china, silver, crystal, and countless trays of every imaginable Middle Eastern pastry. Tears came into my eyes as he motioned us to find a place and be seated. Metropolitan Philip remained standing at his place in the center.

"Brothers," he said with a broad smile, "Welcome home!"

My happiness button finally got pressed!

After the blessing, everyone started in on the coffee, the pastry, and the conversation. But somehow it still wasn't enough. It was like you wanted to run out into the streets to dance and celebrate. But thirty-plus men in clerical garb don't dance with each other (at least not in the *Orthodox* Church they don't). Could we sing, could we crown a king, or hire a brass band?

"What's the problem, Bishop Peter?" asked the Metropolitan. I was sitting immediately across the table from him and obviously wearing my feelings of exuberance on my sleeve.

"I'm so charged up, I want to do something to celebrate. This is magnificent, all of this that you've done. But there must be something we can *do*, something to let loose all this sense of joy. . . ."

"Hans," he called out, motioning the deacon to the

table. "Bring out the cigars!"

The place roared with laughter. It was exactly what the moment called for. Deacon Hans came back into the room with two boxes of huge imported cigars. Men who had never even smoked took one and lit up. It was as if a giant release valve had been activated. A minute or so later, Kathy came back into the room with a new pot of coffee. "Your Eminence!" she said, "It's like an opium den in here."

We howled again. It was as though we had fallen out of character for a few precious moments, and we loved every second of it.

As emotions mellowed over the coffee, dessert, and now cigars, Fr. Gordon Walker made a request. "Your Eminence," he began, "many of us come from backgrounds that have been very pro-Israel. Here we are coming into a Church that has been brought to America by Arab Christians. Take a minute as these depraved men are finishing their cigars [he had one, too, and he *hates* them], and tell us how you view the regathering of the nation of Israel."

It was tragic his answer wasn't taped. For thirty minutes, starting with Abraham in the Old Testament, Metropolitan Philip gave us the most profoundly moving Bible lesson on Israel and the Arab nations I have ever heard. He was careful to clarify the difference between Zionism as a political movement, often exclusivistic and apartheid, and Judaism as a respected nation and faith. I cannot think of an evangelical Christian who would not have waited in line and paid at the door to get in. I came away with a greater desire for peace and justice in the Middle East—both for Israel and the Palestinians—than I had ever known before.

"The Lord be with all of you," the Metropolitan said as he concluded his remarks, "and please give my love to all your people. Let us take the year ahead to get to know each

other. We will look at next summer or, at the latest, next
fall, to begin the chrismations and ordinations to bring
you into the Church."

There is a song which Orthodox Christians sing at
weddings, anniversaries, and most especially during the
Divine Liturgy when the Bishop comes to celebrate. We had
learned the song years earlier, and it had already become a
part of our tradition. As we stood to leave the table, without
a cue, we turned to our paternal friend, and with one voice
sang out "God grant you many years, God grant you many
years, God grant you many, many years!" We sang at the
top of our voices. The whole place dissolved into tears and
embraces. I had never meant the words of a song so much
in my entire life!

On the way to the front door, Fr. Joe Allen, who had
come in during the celebration, grabbed my arm and pulled
me aside.

"I want to ask you something. In December we will be
celebrating the Metropolitan's 20th anniversary in the episcopate. There will be a Hierarchical Liturgy on Sunday
morning, December 9, at the Cathedral in Brooklyn, followed by a banquet on Staten Island. Would you and your
wife come as our guests and represent the EOC?"

The New York Weekend

We decided to come to New York a couple of days early
to Christmas shop in Manhattan. A month or so before we
left, I was on the phone firming up the plane tickets, and
something told me to call our friends, Tom and Lovelace
Howard, in Boston to see if they would want to come down
for a day of shopping on Saturday and dinner in the
evening. "Is this the Lord trying to get through to me?" I
thought to myself. "Naw. The Howards have more going

than they can handle anyway that time of year." I ordered the tickets and made hotel reservations.

The flight into La Guardia landed after dinner, and Marilyn and I took a bus into Manhattan. It was 9:00 when we checked into the hotel, and it was too early to stay put. So we bundled up and walked *everywhere*—to Rockefeller Center to see the skaters and the tree, to Saks to see the animated Christmas windows, to Saint Patrick's Cathedral, up Fifth Avenue to Trump tower—and on back to the hotel.

Saturday was set aside to shop. We decided to start at Saks Fifth Avenue. As we stepped outside our hotel and headed down the street we came upon the Waldorf Astoria. "Let's cut through the lobby and see the Christmas decorations," I said to Marilyn, sensing we were *supposed* to cut through the lobby. We walked through the door, up the escalator, and down the hall to the lobby area. The decorations were all up, and they were beautiful. We took our time, drifting through one end of the lobby to the other and out the door to the street. The crowd outside was shoulder to shoulder, elbow to elbow. I looked ahead down toward the corner and here, making their way down the sidewalk together, were Tom and Lovelace Howard and son Charles!

It was like still another signpost on the journey. "As for me, being on the way," Isaac's servant said, "the LORD led me . . ." (Genesis 24:27). We all stepped back inside the Waldorf in disbelief, caught up on several years of not seeing each other, and made a date for dinner that evening.

Sunday morning came very early. We hailed a cab to the Cathedral and were there just after nine. Orthodox Christians had come from across the country, laity and clergy, including Metropolitan Theodosius and Archbishop Iakovos. Fr. Paul Schneirla gave the homily at the Divine Liturgy. After the service, Fr. Antony Gabriel of Montreal drove us to the celebration banquet on Staten Island. For several hours, we feasted and fellowshiped together, honoring the man we would soon call Saidna (Say-éd-na), the intimate Arabic word for master. Monday was spent with friends at Saint Vladimir's and Tuesday, Marilyn and I kept an appointment with Metropolitan Philip to brief him on our progress over the past three months.

Tuesday held a twofold agenda: lunch and "The Surprise." For in addition to a lovely brass metal tray from the Middle East, Saidna Philip had another Christmas gift for us as well.

"How are the EOC people doing?" he asked as we adjourned to the living room after lunch. "Are they ready to be brought into the Church?"

"They are ready," I assured him, assuming he would suggest the chrismations and ordinations begin at the North American Archdiocesan Convention in Detroit the following summer.

"Good! I will be in California in early February, and we'll begin chrismations and ordinations February 8 at Saint Michael's, Van Nuys," he responded without hesitation.

February 8! That was two months away. One year had been reduced to five months. "That's spectacular," I think I said. Or it was something like that. In two months, some two thousand evangelical pilgrims would complete their journey into Orthodox Christianity.

"Kathy, come in here with the calendar. We're starting the chrismations of the Evangelical Orthodox in February," he called to his secretary in the adjacent room.

The remainder of the afternoon, we planned out the schedule. In the Los Angeles area, most of the EOC members would be chrismated and the clergy ordained as deacons on February 8. The next Sunday at Saint Nicholas Cathedral, the rest of the L.A. area laity would be chrismated and the deacons would be ordained priests. From there, Metropolitan Philip would go up the coast and repeat the process in Santa Cruz, and then on to Nashville for chrismations and ordinations the next weekend.

Bishop Antoun would step in during March to bring our parishes in Jackson, Mississippi, in Memphis, Tennessee, in Gary, Indiana, and our three in Canada into the Church. Finally, the Metropolitan would fly to Anchorage and Seattle to complete the process by early April.

"This way, the entire EOC will be in the bosom of Holy Orthodoxy by Easter," Metropolitan Philip smiled. "My friend, Peter, your journey is almost over—or should I say, your journey is ready to begin."

As we said good-bye, we wished each other a blessed Christmas. There was so much to be grateful for this year. And 1987 would be even better.

On the flight home the following day, I made a list of the people I needed to call. Seventeen parishes had two months to make final plans for hosting one of our new bishops. The courtship was nearly over; the marriage was at hand.

12

ON TO THE THIRD MILLENNIUM

A rchdeacon Hans said it best. "Each of these chrismation and ordination services is like a little Pentecost,"
he remarked during the Divine Liturgy in Nashville as the
people came forward to receive their first communion as
Orthodox Christians.

The service at Saint Michael's, Van Nuys, two weeks
earlier had lasted nearly four hours, as over two hundred
people were chrismated and numerous men ordained to
the diaconate. In fact, the crowd was so large, they removed
all the glass panels on the west side of the sanctuary and set
up a huge rented tent to handle the overflow. "This looks
like a Pentecostal revival," I said to Fr. John Bartke before
the service. In the classical sense of the term, it was.

The first person I met as we walked into the Church
that February morning was Julianna Schmemann, wife of
the late Fr. Alexander Schmemann. She had come all the
way from New York to Los Angeles to witness the event.
Her presence was a highlight for everyone, and I could
scarcely express my appreciation to her for coming.

All of us, EOC clergy and laity, were chrismated at the beginning of the service. Then, during the Liturgy itself, the deacons were ordained—each one personally receiving the laying on of hands by the Metropolitan. The new California parishes represented were Saint Barnabas, Huntington Beach, Fr. Wayne Wilson; Saint Athanasius, Santa Barbara, Fr. Richard Ballew; Saint Timothy, Lompoc, Fr. David Ogan; Saint Athanasius, Sacramento, Fr. Thomas Renfree; and from Nevada, Saint James, Reno, Fr. Timothy McCoy.

Though in the New Testament and for much of Church history there were multiple ordinations, the more recent custom in Orthodoxy has been to ordain only one deacon or presbyter at a service. But there were so many of us, custom gave way to tradition and, as with the Apostle Paul, Metropolitan Philip "laid hands on them" (Acts 19:6) for the grace of the Holy Spirit.

The prayer the bishop prays for each new deacon includes these words:

> Grant that he may love the beauty of Your house, stand before the doors of Your holy Temple, and kindle the lamps in the tabernacle of Your glory. And plant him in Your holy Church like a fruitful olive tree, which brings forth the fruits of righteousness. And make him Your perfect servant at the time of Your Coming, that he may receive the recompense of those who are well-pleasing in Your sight.

We were entering together into the holy order of deacons begun with seven men, including Saint Stephen, the first martyr for Jesus Christ in the newborn Church.

There was one person missing at Saint Michael's that morning. Peggy Thomas was home in Santa Barbara fighting a battle with terminal cancer and was too ill to come. Her family was chrismated, and her husband, Steve, ordained that morning without her. "She's *got* to make it next week," he said as we left the sanctuary. "Pray for her."

After the service, the people at Saint Michael's served us an absolute feast. It's one of several times I admitted part of the reason I turned Orthodox was for the food!

The next Sunday brought more chrismations and the ordination of the deacons to the priesthood at Saint Nicholas Cathedral in Los Angeles, where Fr. Paul Romley is pastor. Dear Bishop Maximos of Pittsburgh was with us, as was Bishop Seraphim of Japan, who years earlier as an evangelical Protestant had graduated from Nyack Bible College. In addition, some twenty Orthodox priests had come in from across North America. Besides the faithful of the Cathedral, scores of friends and parents, including my own, were on hand to witness the glorious event.

It was another Pentecost. The joy of the Lord filled His Temple. As the priests were ordained one by one, Metropolitan Philip prayed:

> The Divine Grace, which always heals that which is infirm, and completes that which is lacking, elevates through the laying on of hands this most devout deacon to be priest.

I knew the moment the words were said I would be called to rely upon the grace which completes what is lacking, for the rest of my life and ministry. The Lord surely does take the baser things of the world to confound the wise.

At the banquet which followed, Bishop Maximos stood to speak. He praised God for His faithfulness to us as pilgrims, and the Metropolitan for his courage and decisiveness in opening to us the door of the Church. It was my joy that afternoon to introduce my parents to these two men of God who had received us all so graciously.

As I stepped outside the back door of the Cathedral to

go to my car, I noticed a van had backed up to the curb area nearby. The sliding door on the side was still open and I looked in as I passed. There, resting and smiling ear to ear was Peggy Thomas. "I made it!" she said. "This was my goal, to be Orthodox."

Just over a month later, Metropolitan Philip wrote Fr. Steve Thomas this letter:

> We have just learned with much sorrow of the falling asleep in Christ of your beloved wife, Peggy. May the Almighty God receive her in His holy mansions, where the faces of the saints shine like the stars of heaven. Beyond this world of suffering and tears, Christ has promised us another world where there is no sickness, sorrow, or pain. Our consolation is that sooner or later, we will join those whom we love beyond the veils of this temporal existence.

On to the Other Parishes

Every Orthodox parish, though sharing the same Lord, same faith, and same hope, still has its own personality. At Saint Peter and Saint Paul Orthodox Church just outside Santa Cruz, pastored by Fr. Weldon Hardenbrook, the personality trait is enthusiasm. It shows up in how the priests pray in the services and how the people sing. Over five hundred people were chrismated there by Metropolitan Philip just three days after the Sunday at Saint Nicholas. I honestly thought heaven might open up and receive us all as the congregation stood to sing "God Grant You Many Years" to the Metropolitan.

The next day we boarded the plane for Nashville to bring in the people and clergy of Saint Ignatius', Franklin, served by Fr. Gordon Walker, and Saint Stephen's, Atlanta, pastored by Fr. Andrew Moore.

In the following month, March of 1987, our parishes, including Saint Peter's, Jackson, Mississippi; Saint John's, Memphis; and Holy Resurrection, Gary, Indiana welcomed Bishop Antoun on two successive weekends, and experienced the same Spirit-filled joy and gladness as the others. Three more EOC bishops—Clark Henderson, Dale Autrey, and Gregory Rogers, the pastors of these parishes—were made priests. Later in the month, the Bishop flew to Saskatoon in central Canada to chrismate the faithful and ordain the clergy there. By month's end Fr. Daniel Matheson's parish in Ottawa, Holy Epiphany; Saint Vincent's in Saskatoon under Fr. Bernard Funk; and Saint Andrew's in nearby Borden under Fr. Larry Reinheimer were Orthodox.

The last two stops were in early April: Anchorage, Alaska to bring in Saint John's of suburban Eagle River, pastored by Fr. Harold Dunaway; and finally Seattle, Washington to bring in Fr. Joseph Copeland's parish, Holy Cross of Yakima, and Saint Paul's of Seattle which had been pastored by Frs. Kenneth Berven and Melvin Gimmaka, and then by Fr. David Anderson.

I was to meet Metropolitan Philip on the first Wednesday in April in Anchorage. Kathy Meyer called a few days beforehand with word that the airline had to schedule him in on Tuesday. Fr. Harold met him and Archdeacon Hans at the airport and drove them out to the community in Eagle River.

"When Saidna Philip stepped inside the Church," Fr. Harold told me the next day, "he said, 'This is a Cathedral.' " The congregation was called together that night at the Metropolitan's request, and the Church was consecrated as Saint John the Evangelist Cathedral. The people were speechless. They had designed and built the Church three years earlier with their own hands. The building preceded them into Orthodoxy by one day!

There was a sidelight to the services in Alaska. On the second day, just after lunch, eight of us, including the Metropolitan, had been invited to take a two-hour sightseeing flight over Mt. McKinley and several glacial areas. We arrived on time at the nearby airport to board the flight, but it never arrived. The plane went down late that morning, tragically killing the two pilots. We decided to make the trip the following day, knowing that our times are in God's hands. "This is the most beautiful flight I've ever taken," Metropolitan Philip remarked as we approached majestic Mt. McKinley.

Friday came, and it was on to Seattle. The same joy was present there, and though we were tired, it was sad to see the festive process end. "I'm going to miss seeing you so often," I told Archdeacon Hans as we left for the airport.

The National Convention

The next summer in Detroit, Metropolitan Philip welcomed us home publicly at the National Convention: "Ladies and Gentlemen, we are celebrating this year an event which did not happen in the remote past, but rather a few months ago," he began.

He told about our initial meeting with the Patriarch in Los Angeles and then turned to the meeting with the EOC synod on September 5, 1986:

> After four hours of intensive theological discussion, something happened which I will never forget. Bishop Gordon Walker of Tennessee broke down and, with tears in his eyes, said to us, "Brothers, we have been knocking on Orthodox doors for ten years, but to no avail. Now, we have come to your doorsteps, seeking the Holy Catholic and Apostolic Faith. If you do not accept us, where do we go from here?"

I was deeply touched and moved by the sincerity of Bishop Walker and, from that moment on, I had no doubt whatsoever that such a dialogue, baptized with tears, would be crowned with heavenly joy.

Later in his remarks, the Metropolitan told of his response to the chrismation services throughout North America:

I wish I could go beyond words to describe to you the joy which I experienced as I was chrismating these little children of the Evangelical Orthodox faithful. Every experience I had was like a chapter from the Book of Acts. I felt as if the Church was recapturing her apostolic spirit and rediscovering, once again, her missionary dimension.

There is a misconception among some of us Orthodox that the Orthodox Church does not proselytize. This is the furthest thing from the truth. Can you imagine where the Church would be if Peter and Paul, Philip and Andrew, and the rest of the Apostles did not proselytize? What America needs today, especially after the collapse of the electronic pulpit, is an Orthodox evangelism based on the true interpretation of the Scripture, the apostolic and patristic teachings, and the liturgical and sacramental life of the Church.

Once again, from the depth of my heart, I say to the Evangelical Orthodox, "Welcome Home!"

The Beginning

The Order of Saint Ignatius is a support group of well over 1000 people within the Antiochian Archdiocese which underwrites special projects. One of them is a twenty-two-minute video presentation called "Welcome Home" which captures on film the entrance of the EOC into the Orthodox Church. At the close of the film, when you would expect to see THE END on the screen, it says, instead, THE BEGINNING. I believe those words are prophetic.

Within a few months of our reception into the Orthodox Church, hundreds more have come home to Orthodoxy. New missions have begun in several American cities—places like Fargo, North Dakota; Salt Lake City, Utah; East Lansing, Michigan; Bloomington, Indiana; Beaver Falls, Pennsylvania; and Wheaton, Illinois. In addition, inquiries come in, sometimes several in one day, from pastors who love Christ and His Church and are seeking the fullness of Orthodox worship and faith.

Many of these are evangelical Protestants who have considered Orthodox Christianity for years, but who were afraid it was too ethnic for them. Others are Episcopalian, mainline Protestant, or Roman Catholic, godly men who are frustrated because every time they turn around, the doctrinal ground under their feet has shifted. They all are seeking doctrinal, liturgical, and ecclesiastical roots.

Another visible center of interest has been Christian college and seminary campuses. Invitations have come, and presentations have been given at a number of such institutions, often with the support of the administration. Schools that would have instantly rejected an Orthodox priest twenty years ago—and I would have been part of the rejection process—are today taking a serious, second look at this ancient faith. Why?

In the last book of the Old Testament—in fact, it's the last verse in the Old Testament—an inspired prediction was set down. God promised that He would turn "the hearts of the children to their fathers" (Malachi 4:6). The people of God share a common hunger to find the founders of their faith, the Church that Jesus Christ established through His Apostles and the Fathers of the Church. Malachi tells us this will occur before the "great and dreadful day of the Lord" (Malachi 4:5).

When the Incarnate God, our Lord Jesus Christ, came to earth the first time, it was the people who took the Law and Prophets seriously who recognized Him and followed Him. What about His Second Coming—will we know Him? Will we be prepared? Jesus warns that some, who say they are, will not be.

Today, much of Christendom is shattered. Large numbers of confessing Christians have left the faith in one degree or other. Believers are orphaned and isolated from their roots. As tragic as this is, remember that God uses even the wrath of men to praise Him. For out of this apostasy comes a hunger for the fullness of the New Testament faith, for new life in Christ, for the worship of the Holy Trinity, for the Church herself.

What is it that we who are Orthodox Christians want? What is our vision, our desire? Simply this: We want to be *the* Church for all seriously committed Christian people in the English-speaking world. Christians in North America, for example, have had the opportunity to decide if they want to be Roman Catholic, Baptist, Lutheran, Presbyterian, Methodist, or even Independent. Very few have been given the chance to decide if they would like to be Orthodox. We wish to make that choice available and to urge people to become part of this original Church of Jesus Christ.

Repeatedly, in the Book of Revelation, Jesus says, "He who has an ear, let him hear what the Spirit says to the Churches." I believe that in these days, the Holy Spirit is issuing a clarion call to the people of God: Children, come home to the faith of your fathers, to your roots in Christendom, to the green pastures and still waters of the Church that has stood the test of time.

As pre-Orthodox Christians we had the right Savior, though we've come to know Him better, together with God the Father and God the Holy Spirit. We had the right Bible, and have come to know it even better. But we had overlooked that enormous missing factor—the right Church. The Spirit and the Bride have beckoned us, and we have gladly come.

This is the Treasure we have found. And we dare not hide it.

Fr. James Meena was right that day at Saint Nicholas Cathedral. Our fathers embraced this Orthodox Christian faith and brought it to America. Now it's our turn to bring America—and the West—to Orthodox Christianity. On to the Third Millennium!

EPILOGUE

SIX YEARS LATER

November, 1992

I t is difficult to believe, but at this writing, nearly six years have transpired since the events chronicled in the preceding pages took place.

When Metropolitan Philip chrismated us back in 1987, renaming this group of former Lutherans, Pentecostals, Baptists, Independents, and people from a host of other backgrounds, the "Antiochian Evangelical Orthodox Mission" (AEOM), he gave us the specific commission to bring the fullness of the Orthodox faith to that huge segment of North America which had never before given it even passing consideration.

I still remember clearly receiving an incredibly diverse array of messages coming in from all sectors of Christendom as we began our approach towards the Antiochian Archdiocese. Some were welcoming us home and preparing the festivities for our arrival. Others were frantically trying to wave us off, warning of impending disaster.

Predictably, those with an historic awareness of the One, Holy, Catholic, and Apostolic Church cheered us on, thrilled with the prospect of at least one less division in Christendom. But others of an independent religious bent warned we would atrophy, that we would lose our cutting edge in evangelism. Even some Orthodox people cautioned us to beware of getting swallowed up in cultural ethnicism.

Those who took part in our journey will remember, as will you who have read the story, that the entrance of the former EOC into the Antiochian Orthodox Archdiocese was a series of joyful, glorious, and holy Eucharistic liturgies conducted over the course of two months in seven different North American cities—Los Angeles to Nashville, Gary to Anchorage—bringing in seventeen parishes in all. The new relationship with the Archdiocese began on a note of great hope. "This is the brightest moment of my life," Metropolitan Philip said in an interview. "I have invested so much hope in the AEOM as a movement."

But is that investment paying off?

New Orthodox Missions

The work of the AEOM in the past six years has been to find ways to fulfill that commission given to us by Metropolitan Philip. We have sought to reach out to the non-Orthodox—Christians and unbelievers alike—through preaching, teaching, and literature, and have found ourselves making a home in the Orthodox Church for already existing Christian congregations. Regarding the latter, in every case the pastor and/or people have sought us out and initiated the contact. An incredible number of pastors have asked for information on how to enter the Orthodox Church, most of them for the same reasons that we pursued Orthodox Christianity.

Because of our background in evangelicalism and campus ministry, we have sought wherever possible to acquaint evangelicals and college students with Orthodoxy. In Chicago, for instance, we chose to begin our mission near Wheaton College. The school graciously rented us a room in Pierce Chapel, and we undertook the challenge of communicating the Orthodox faith to evangelical students. Holy Transfiguration Mission in Wheaton has grown out of that effort. A former independent evangelical congregation near East Lansing, now Saint James, has launched an on-campus outreach at Michigan State.

Significant numbers of inquiries have recently come in from traditional Episcopalian clergy, laity, and parishes who are finding solace in the unchangeable faith of the Orthodox Church. In addition to the individuals and families who have come, priests and portions of their flock have come as well, including two parishes in the Denver, Colorado area, one in Fort Worth, Texas, and one in suburban Milwaukee, Wisconsin.

Altogether, fifteen new mission parishes have started since our entry in 1987, nearly doubling the number of "convert" congregations. Another fifteen or so are making preparations to do the same within the coming year.

The Print Media

In the past five years, we have been privileged to produce a number of books and articles which have generated unpredictably strong response among readers. Father Jack Sparks added explanatory notes for Protestants to an excellent translation of *The Apostolic Fathers*, under the editorship of Robert M. Grant, which has been recently republished. This volume has introduced many new people to the early Church. Father Jon Braun's *Divine Energy* and the original edition of *Becoming Orthodox* have stirred new interest in this ancient faith. The book *Coming Home: Why*

Protestant Clergy are Becoming Orthodox tells the story of eighteen pastors who have entered the Orthodox Church in recent years. The readership of our *Again* magazine continues to expand steadily, both here in North America, and even in a small but growing number of countries overseas.

Shortly after our entrance into the Church the national print media began taking notice, asking if a movement toward Orthodoxy was underway. Articles appeared in the *Los Angeles Times* and *Atlantic Monthly*. Soon an interview was published in *U.S. News and World Report*, followed up by a second article on Orthodox Christianity a year later. Several Christian magazines, mainly from the evangelical and charismatic sector, including *Faith and Renewal* and *Christianity Today*, carried very positive articles and interviews.

Several months prior to our fifth anniversary in the Orthodox Church, David Heim, managing editor of the *Christian Century*, asked me to write a piece, and we agreed the theme would center on our five-year report. Since I came from the conservative wing of Protestantism, I was interested in what reader response might be. The article, published in March, 1992, brought in the largest volume of mail I had ever received from a magazine piece of any kind. Most of the correspondents were traditional Christian pastors in the mainline denominations asking if there were a place for them in Orthodoxy.

I discovered something else in relationship to *Christian Century*. The day I turned in my article, in January of 1992, Fr. Bill Caldaroni, our priest in Wheaton, and I were invited to join the staff for lunch and conversation. On the way into the room where we were to meet, I noticed a whole series of "in-boxes" stacked up against the wall— maybe thirty of them. My eye caught the first few labels:

Presbyterian, Methodist, Jewish, Roman Catholic. . . . Immediately I stopped reading and turned to Fr. Bill. "See those boxes? This is where the religious media packets and news releases come into the editorial offices. I'll bet you anything there's no Orthodox box."

We looked and the closest we came under "O" was "Other."

After a brief skirmish with my own anger at the magazine for "ignoring us," I realized precisely why our box was missing. We Orthodox do perhaps the worst job of any religious body in America of communicating with those outside the Church. This is the best-kept secret on the continent, to our shame.

In early 1993, Thomas Nelson will publish volume one of the *Orthodox Study Bible* (New Testament and Psalms), which we, together with numerous Orthodox scholars and theologians worldwide, have labored on for three years. Simply written, with voluminous notes, we anticipate this volume will both attract Orthodox Christians to serious Bible study and introduce others to Orthodoxy "verse by verse."

Evangelism Efforts

In 1988, we began the annual Orthodox Missions and Evangelism Conferences held each Labor Day weekend. To my knowledge this was an Orthodox "first," as several hundred clergy and laypeople—Orthodox and non-Orthodox—have come for training. A number of new missions have resulted, and the commitment to evangelism on the part of Orthodox Christians is visibly growing.

Fr. Joseph Fester, who heads up evangelism and Church growth for the OCA, joined us for the 1990 Conference, and his enthusiasm produced cosponsorship of the event with the OCA in 1991. Mr. Jack Hill of the Greek Orthodox Archdiocese was an observer that same year, resulting in cosponsorship with the Greek Archdiocese in 1992. Our joy at this new effort of Orthodox unity was heightened when Archbishop Iakovos appointed Bishop Maximos to represent him. At this level, there has come renewed solidarity between the OCA, the Greek Orthodox, and ourselves. Not only is the Conference growing in effectiveness, but it has moved from being an Antiochian effort to an American Pan-Orthodox movement.

In strategy sessions with Metropolitan Philip, we in the AEOM have set as our goal 500 new Orthodox parishes in North America by the end of the year 2000.

And while we're on the subject of evangelism, we have recently been given the opportunity to preach the Gospel in a very dramatic way. In August, 1992, four of us convert priests were asked to go on a two-week mission trip to Romania. Frs. Gregory Rogers, John Reeves, and Roman Braga as interpreter were one team, Frs. David Ogan, Dan Suciu, interpreter, and myself were the other. We preached to crowds ranging in size from a few hundred to 10,000 to 35,000 to 100,000, and the fact that we were Americans and relative newcomers to Orthodoxy was a giant plus. Many, including ourselves, made renewed commitments to Jesus Christ, and we all want to go back to Romania.

Discovering Worship and the Spiritual Life

Speaking very personally, though I suspect my situation in the 1980s was representative of many of us, I did not come to Orthodoxy because I was attracted by a new potential for spiritual life. I came because I was convinced biblically and historically that the teachings of the Church were correct, that this was the true faith. In the process I discovered the true spiritual depth of the Orthodox faith.

Back in 1950, A.W. Tozer, who taught at Moody Bible Institute in Chicago, preached a sermon so memorable it was transcribed into a booklet still in print over forty years later. His title was "The Missing Jewel of Evangelicalism," which he identified as true worship. Unfortunately, the jewel is still missing.

For nearly two decades of my life, I had evaluated worship in categories such as: Does it hold me? Is it exciting and invigorating? Is it fresh and creative? Does it meet my needs? But as we studied the roots of Christian worship, starting way back in the Old Testament, those categories, of course, were not there. Instead, we were confronted with such questions as: Is this in spirit and in truth? Is it patterned after things in the heavens? Does it glorify God? I embraced liturgical and sacramental worship not for its exhilaration or ecstasy, but because it was right. It is as though I have come home to worship.

The reality of this worship has opened for us the door to a fullness of salvation we did not know was there. It has brought about a sense of wholeness for our people we did not have before. Functioning together as a corporate priest-hood, a Eucharistic community, had been an aspect of salvation omitted and overlooked in our earlier days. And that "mystic sweet communion with those whose rest is won" brings an element of spiritual life which is beyond description. I knew those words by heart and had utterly missed their meaning. Now I'm becoming acquainted with the saints who have gone on before—not just as names to be remembered, but as cherished friends.

The farther we have gone on this journey—the more we have read, encountered, and experienced Orthodox spirituality firsthand—the more we have learned to appreciate its great depth and beauty. The soil here is rich and fertile; there is room to put down roots and grow for a lifetime.

Admittedly, we are the new kids on the block, we have made our mistakes along the way, and have lots of "growing up" to do. You simply do not arrive at spiritual maturity overnight, or over the course of six years. But even in our early faltering steps, the balance of discipline and freedom, of physical reality and mystical experience, and especially the wonderful emphasis upon prayer as a day-by-day, moment-by-moment way of life has been very blessed indeed.

A final point under spiritual life must be made regarding the Scriptures themselves. Though I had struggled not to do it, so much of my handling of the Bible had been as an end in itself, not the means to the end of knowing God and growing in a relationship with Him. With my rationalistic bent, it was so easy to treat the Bible as a cadaver to be spread out, dissected, analyzed.

The most arresting change for me is that in Orthodoxy the Scriptures are used liturgically. We *pray* the Psalms, for example, we do not merely read or study them. We journey with Jesus Christ through the Gospels into the drama of salvation connected to the cycle of the Church year. The Bible is the book of the Church, not just of the individual. In many ways, the life of the Church forces me to go back and take seriously the verses I *didn't* underline. There is an Orthodox sense of Scripture which, honestly, is still dawning on me.

How Has It Been in an "Ethnic" Church?

Just as Ruth the Moabitess realized some 3000 years ago, when you follow God you also take up with His people. So we also have embraced those incredible Middle Eastern people who have made a home for us in the Orthodox faith.

One of the unusual things about Americans becoming Orthodox is the fear people have—and I believe it's there on both sides—that the one culture will force the other culture into its mold. Nobody likes to talk it through, because even to introduce the subject implicitly suggests racism.

But as the day of unity approached, you could occasionally hear our side worry aloud, "I sure hope they don't try to make Arabs out of us!" But the other culture was heard asking more than once concerning us, "What if they try to make the Church Protestant?"

There are few things in life that turn out better than you hope, and our reception by the people of the Antiochian Archdiocese has been one of them. I will not say that there were—and in some cases still are—no barriers or obstacles to be overcome. I will say dogmatically, however, that the wedding of these two cultures has worked. Differences in style, temperament, and tradition have fit well together to foster unity and respect. Some of the exchanges have been downright humorous.

One day I had occasion to call a veteran Antiochian priest in New York. His teenage son answered the phone. When I asked for his dad, he said he was out. "Who should I say called?" he asked.

"I'm Fr. Peter Gillquist," I told him.

"Oh, you're the one who shouts when he preaches!" the young man offered.

Okay, he got me. While my message is Orthodox, I still deliver it as an evangelical. Frankly, I am enthused about being Orthodox, and I'll probably never conform to the cultural decibel of traditional Eastern preaching, though I suspect Saint John Chrysostom didn't either.

As time has gone by and we have grown accustomed to the external differences which exist between our varied cultures, we have come to learn that in Christ "there is neither Greek nor Jew, circumcised nor uncircumcised, barbarian, Scythian, slave nor free, but Christ is all and in all" (Colossians 3:11). As His spiritual sons and daughters we can appreciate, rather than fear, our differences. During these six years, we have laughed together, worked together, at times butted heads together. But in all things, we have truly grown to love one another as brothers and sisters in Christ.

Having said that, there remain great challenges. I question why it is that the people in a given North American Orthodox parish can read the paper, trade securities, and order a Big Mac all in English, and then insist the services the following Sunday be in Greek, Slavonic, or Arabic—especially when their kids can't grasp a word of it. Or, why it is that we still have three Orthodox bishops in the same city, each representing a different jurisdiction. With this backdrop, how do we effectively and broadly communicate this ancient holy faith to modern secular America?

The tasks out there which need to be completed are legion. But after living in our new home of Orthodoxy since 1987, we are all more than grateful to be here.

Why We Became Orthodox

A question which is put to me repeatedly as I visit and speak with non-Orthodox Christians throughout this continent is: "What was it that finally motivated you to take that step? What ultimately prompted you to leave the Protestant world behind in favor of the distant shores of Orthodoxy?"

I can honestly say, most of us were not drawn here by any gross disenchantment with the evangelical movement, nor by an incurable preoccupation with the smells and bells attendant with Orthodox worship. As I said at the outset, the change came for us when we stopped trying to judge and reevaluate Church history, and for once invited Church history to judge and evaluate us.

We were already firmly committed to the inspiration of the Scriptures, the deity of Christ, and the Great Commission of our Lord. To identify the Church of the first century in the pages of the New Testament posed no problem for us. Our questions were: 1) Where did that New Testament Church *go* in history? and 2) How did our own expression of Christianity measure up to the pattern which had been set down in the centuries *following* the Book of Acts?

To our amazement, we found the Church of the first millennium to be an undivided unity. Here and there some early heretical groups had exited, to be sure, and there were the difficult situations involving the Nestorians and the Monophysites. But within the Church itself there was unity of *doctrine* as the apostolic faith was guarded by the great Ecumenical Councils. There was a basic shape or order of liturgical *worship*. And the *government* of the Church was unified under her five great patriarchal centers. Instead of asking if Christian forebears like Anselm, Augustine, Athanasius, and Chrysostom were in our Church, we began to ask if we were in theirs!

The more we listened to the ancient apologists for the faith, cross-referencing their writings with the Scriptures, the more we understood that for them, everything centered upon the doctrines of the Holy Trinity and the Incarnation of the Son of God. In this light, issues which had troubled us as evangelicals—sacrament, liturgy, the honoring of Mary and the saints, icons, and the historic continuity of the episcopacy—began to come into focus.

So for us, Orthodox Christianity was not a "leap of faith." It was rather a coming home. As with the multitudes of faithful in ages past we decided to act: to enter into liturgical worship, to receive the sacraments, to bless her who bore the Savior of our souls, to pray with icons, to seek out the watch-care of bishops.

A Movement of the Spirit

Early in 1992, I was with His Grace, Bishop Antoun, in Bethesda, Maryland, as he chrismated and ordained the laity and clergy from two brand-new Orthodox missions in Wilmington, Delaware and Virginia Beach, Virginia. In his homily that weekend he said, "A new movement of the Holy Spirit began in the Orthodox Church in 1987."

These past six years have been exciting and rewarding. Besides the normal growth fostered in the Church through the centuries, this new move has brought a change involving thousands of Protestant Christians discovering Orthodox Christianity for the first time, hundreds of them entering the Church.

Many who read this book have made this same journey. If you are still in that process, let me assure you: there is a home for you in this ancient faith. To those who are independent Christians, God offers community and historic connectedness. To those whose Christian experience centers in Bible study, add to your biblical knowledge the reality of worship and sacrament. To those in a place where there is a move away from the center of apostolic doctrine, the Church offers you the unchanging faith "once for all delivered to the saints" (Jude 3).

The truth is, if we who came from the largely pop-evangelical culture of the Sixties as walk-ons into Orthodoxy can make it here with gratitude and joy, *anyone* can! We have never been asked to alter our nationalities, our zeal for evangelism, or our love of the Scriptures, or to deny the mercy and gifts God has given us in days gone by.

Instead, we have filled the many missing places of our Christian lives with the glories of Orthodoxy. And we have dropped that which was not true to the holy faith.

Just as Metropolitan Philip promised us in 1986, the Holy Spirit *has* led us "into the right land." We look forward to the continuing task of introducing North America to the riches of this historic faith.

FOR FURTHER READING

Holy Scripture
The Orthodox Study Bible, Vol. I: New Testament and Psalms (Nashville, TN: Thomas Nelson, Inc., 1993).

Antiochian Orthodox Christian Archdiocese
Peter E. Gillquist, *Metropolitan Philip: His Life and Dreams* (Nashville, TN: Thomas Nelson, 1991).

Metropolitan Philip Saliba, *Feed My Sheep* (Crestwood, NY: St. Vladimir's Seminary Press, 1987).

Church History
Gregory Rogers, *Apostolic Succession* (Ben Lomond, CA: Conciliar Press, 1989).

Jack N. Sparks, ed., *The Apostolic Fathers* (Minneapolis, MN: Light and Life, 1978).

Timothy Ware, *The Orthodox Church* (Baltimore, MD: Penguin Books, 1993).

Faith and Worship
Jon E. Braun, *Divine Energy: The Orthodox Path to Christian Victory* (Ben Lomond, CA: Conciliar Press, 1991).

Anthony Coniaris, *Introducing the Orthodox Church* (Minneapolis, MN: Light and Life, 1982).

Peter E. Gillquist, ed., *Coming Home: Why Protestant Clergy Are Becoming Orthodox* (Ben Lomond, CA: Conciliar Press, 1992).

John Meyendorff, *Living Tradition* (Crestwood, NY: St. Vladimir's Seminary Press, 1978).

Archbishop Paul, *The Faith We Hold* (Crestwood, NY: St. Vladimir's Seminary Press, 1980).

Alexander Schmemann, *For the Life of the World* (Crestwood, NY: St. Vladimir's Seminary Press, 1973).

_____, *Of Water and the Spirit* (Crestwood, NY: St. Vladimir's Seminary Press, 1974).

_____, *The Eucharist* (Crestwood, NY: St. Vladimir's Seminary Press, 1987).

These books and additional information concerning the Orthodox Church are available through Conciliar Press, P.O. Box 76, Ben Lomond, CA 95005; (408) 336-5118 or (800) 967-7377. Please write for a free catalog.

ABOUT THE AUTHOR

Peter E. Gillquist is an archpriest in the Antiochian Orthodox Christian Archdiocese of North America and chairman of the Department of Missions and Evangelism for the archdiocese. He is publisher of Conciliar Press/ *Again* Magazine, and serves on the Evangelism Commission of the National Council of Churches.

Fr. Peter was educated at the University of Minnesota, Dallas Theological Seminary, and Wheaton College Graduate School. In the 1960s, he was regional director of Campus Crusade for Christ, later senior book editor at Thomas Nelson Publishers. He has authored numerous books including *Love is Now* and *The Physical Side of Being Spiritual* (Zondervan), and *Designed for Holiness* (Servant). Most recently he edited *Coming Home* (Conciliar Press).

Other Stories of people who have embraced the Orthodox Faith:

*Note: prices listed were current as of January, 2001. Prices are subject to change. When ordering directly from publishers, please enclose additional funds to cover tax and postage & handling.

COMING HOME
Edited by Fr. Peter E. Gillquist (Conciliar Press) $8.95
Eighteen testimonies from former Protestant clergy of diverse backgrounds—Presbyterian, Baptist, United Methodist, charismatic, Anglican, and more—who are uniting under the banner of the One Holy and Apostolic Church.

ANGLICAN-ORTHODOX PILGRIMAGE
Edited by Franklin Billerbeck (Conciliar Press) $4.50
Why are so many Anglicans considering entrance into the Orthodox Church? Written entirely by former Anglicans/Episcopalians, this book contains a strong apologetic for the Orthodox Faith as well as personal testimonies by those who have recently made the pilgrimage.

FACING EAST
By Frederica Mathewes-Green (Harper San Francisco) hardcover, $22.00
Frederica depicts the living experience of Orthodoxy throughout the liturgical year, through the joys and sorrows of her own small mission parish in its third year of existence. This endearingly personal, yet surprisingly universal journal provides an excellent introduction to "nuts and bolts" Orthodoxy for the inquirer, as well as a moving and uplifting read for those already within the fold.

OUR HEARTS' TRUE HOME
Edited by Virginia Nieuwsma (Conciliar Press) $12.95
Presents fourteen warm, inspiring stories of women coming into the Orthodox Faith. These women come from a wide variety of backgrounds, yet there's a common thread: no matter how they struggled, their journeys are infused with the love and mercy of God.

A FAITH FULFILLED
By Fr. Michael Harper (Conciliar Press) $13.95
Michael Harper, known to many American Christians as a longtime leader in the evangelical and charismatic movements in the Church of England, now comes before us in a new role: as a convert to the Orthodox Church.

To request a Conciliar Press catalog, place a credit card order, or to obtain current ordering information, please **call Conciliar Press at (800) 967-7377 or (831) 336-5118, or log on to our website: www.conciliarpress.com**